The Mindful Traveler

The Mindful Traveler

A Guide to Journaling and Transformative Travel

Jim Currie

Foreword by Phil Cousineau

OPEN COURT

Chicago and La Salle, Illinois

Cartoons by Scot Ritchie.
Book design by John Grandits.

To order books from Open Court, call 1-800-815-2280.

Open Court Publishing Company is a division of Carus Publishing Company.

©2000 by Carus Publishing Company

First printing 2000

Printed and bound in the United States of America.

Library of Congress Cataloging-in-Publication Data
Currie, J. D. (Jim D.)
The mindful traveler: a guide to journaling and transformative travel/Jim Currie.
p. c.m.
Includes bibliographical references and index.
ISBN 0-8126-9421-X (pbk.)
1. Travel—Religious aspects. 2. Diaries—Authorship—Religious aspects. 3. Travel—Religious aspects—Buddhism. 4. Diaries—Authorship—Religious aspects—Buddhism. 5. Travel. I. Title.

BL628.8 C87 2000
291.4'46—dc21

00-055765

To Myra, Gigi and Chris for Your
Vision, Faith and Inspiration

Contents

Foreword

*I*n the spring of 2000 I drove with a friend down the winding stonewalled roads south of Dublin to the mysterious ruins of Glendalough, a sixth-century monastic settlement. While there I hiked along the ancient paths that meander around the old churches, graveyard, and round tower, and learned from an Irish guide about a local ritual that goes straight to the heart of wise travel.

In the nearby Wicklow Gap there is an old stone pathway known as Saint Kevin's Road. At the ancient crossroads where Kevin's Road joins the Glendalough road is an old stone incised with a cross. It marks the place where travelers have gathered for centuries to pray, celebrate, or simply marvel at the beauty of the valley around them. According to custom, travelers have always paused at this crossroads before descending down to the holy grounds, so they can reflect on their long journey, perhaps even share some stories with fellow travelers about the obstacles they met along the way, or discuss their hopes about the curative powers of the famous relics at the monastery. The crossroad also marked the time and place to reaffirm one's purpose for taking the journey. Stopping there meant a chance to ask, "Where is my journey really leading? What blessings do I seek? What gifts am I bringing with me?"

I've come to think of this contemplative state of mind as the "pilgrim mood" or "traveler's reverie." The practice allows for ritual reflection on the deeper meaning of travel, and a chance to express gratitude for the adventure in which we find ourselves.

There is a comparable physical place and psychological state of mind to be discovered at the threshold of virtually all signficant destinations. But the crossroads that lead to Glendalough are symbolic to me of the crossroads that travelers now encounter on every journey. The question is whether there are any ritual practices anymore that allow us to choose the right road, the right way to travel.

Tourism has become very powerful in our time, actually overtaking the armaments industry as the number one business in the world. Every alert traveler knows the ambiguous influence their own presence brings, for tourism can be either a creative or a destructive force. One of the great questions of our time is how to travel more conscientiously, and how to adapt popular destinations for the onslaught of visitors.

There was a conference in Prague in the mid-Nineties that echoed this concern. During the proceedings the following question was asked of the speakers, "What change would you most like to see come about in the twenty-first century?" The scientist Rupert Sheldrake startled the audience by saying, "I would change tourism into pilgrimage, help tourists become pilgrims."

In that pithy response Sheldrake acknowledged not only that travel is now a force to be reckoned with, but that it can be transformed.

In this regard we are at an historical crossroads. One road leads to escapism and exploitation, what we might call mindless travel; the other leads down the road of respect and attentiveness, the ancient way of the pilgrim, or what Buddhists have long called mindful travel.

The spirit of the crossroads en route to Glendalough and the tone and tenor of Sheldrake's comment are both at the heart of this new work by Jim Currie, *The Mindful Traveler*. In these pages Currie suggests ways to help travelers move beyond the aggressive model of mere tourism to that of mindful traveling, by which he means the practice of being alert to your own inner life while on the road, in addition to the dignity and wonder of the new world we are encountering. His book is chock-full of reminders to those who may want to follow in the footsteps of pious travelers walking to Jerusalem, Bodh Gaya, or Basho's Far Province, but is also instructive for ordinary travelers who only want to be more respectful and aware as they tread the back roads of Galway, Venice, or Gettysburg. What all these travelers share in common is similar to that of the travelers poised at the crossroads above Glendalough. They pause and take in the marvel of the moment. This is harder than it sounds, yet all you need to do, as the Buddhist monk Thich Nhat Hanh has said, is "enjoy each step you take."

The Mindful Traveler aims to support just this spirit of attentiveness. The author invokes what he calls the traveler's own Buddha nature, the spontaneously true self. His goal is to teach travelers how to enliven any form of travel, even the humblest of vacations. But he is careful to emphasize that this takes discipline, warning that "Mindfulness is next to impossible if you don't provide the space." So he suggests ways to develop the time and space for a different sensibility. His methods include journal-keeping, mandala or spiritual map drawing, visualization exercises for staying clear about one's intentions, and practical suggestions for taking care of personal property, avoiding illness, and meeting people.

The essayist Pico Iyer writes that the most satisfying travel is attentive, as if we were in love. We are moving in a a heightened state of awareness, sensitivity, spontaneity when we travel passionately, and in this state we are saved from what he calls abstraction and ideology. Currie is aware of the danger of being overprepared and so reminds the reader that his suggestions are all simple touchstones for staying clear about the purpose of the journey. The metaphor is similar to that of crossroad stones that encouraged travelers to stop and reflect on the reasons why they accepted the great challenge of the journey in the first place.

After reading these pages, it will soon be time for your own journey. It may be helpful to recall that the Buddha's last words were an injunction to his followers to simply, "Walk on."

Phil Cousineau

San Francisco
June, 2000

Introduction

*E*very year increasing numbers of people journey to far-flung places to renew themselves through travel. In the process they often discover that the best trips are those that affirm something about spirit and self-identity, that deepen connections with others, that provide opportunities for learning, self-expression, or making a contribution to a healthier planet or world community.

This book addresses these interests by providing a quick and efficient journal-keeping method for recording daily events, dramas, and mindsets. The approach allows you to capture observations and thoughts soon after they occur, and then bring greater insight to them later when you have more time. Drawing upon Buddhism, Taoism, and other Eastern traditions, the method may be used to heighten self-awareness and promote opportunities for discovery, adventure, and meaningful personal experiences.

The book is liberally spiced with practical ways to deal with the impediments of travel. Some are quick fixes, intended to get you over and around the potholes; others are a bit more elaborate, requiring attention to state of mind and what the Buddha called "mindfulness." Wherever possible I try to be specific and concrete.

Suggestions are offered for protecting personal property, preventing illness, meeting the right people, picking compatible partners, traveling smoothly with your mates, and packing light both physically and emotionally. Prescriptions are based upon my own mistakes and what I have learned from seasoned travelers who have mastered the art of traveling light and leaving shallow footprints.

For those who are more ambitious, who are interested in more than troubleshooting and trouble avoidance, this book shows how to electrify your trip with mindfulness—how to tap the power of higher intention and heartfelt desire for a trip you won't soon forget. Toward this end, the book suggests ways to activate your resourcefulness as an explorer, healer, mystic, communicator, and rational problem-solver. These are all aspects of Buddha nature which you can tap to enliven and deepen your vacation, business, and adventure travel. (I will introduce you to eight different Buddha archetypes which you can draw on for a more powerful trip.)

If this is your interest, familiarize yourself with the overall technique, its basic steps and logic, then follow the steps in a systematic way, as described in chapter 1. You will soon learn how to call out your own sleeping Buddha nature to guide you down your travel path, be it close or far from home. Practicing the method with resilience, openness, and sensitivity, you are apt to spark powerful synchronicities, meet the right people at just the right time, and enhance your trip in ways you couldn't predict in advance.

Whatever your interests, you will get the most out of this guide by first reading it for essence. On first pass browse through the various chapters to take in the arc of the method and how it relates inner reflection to outer experience. Later, go back to those sections which speak to your special interests and dig more deeply.

For those who decide to follow the method in stepwise fashion, don't get bogged down in the rigors of specific substeps. If you find yourself laboring joylessly, move on. This is particularly important when you are getting started and are called upon to define personal touchstones, objectives, or travel strategy. Fundamental beliefs and intentions are often difficult to express on first pass. Allow your subconscious to work on them while you are moving forward through the other chapters.

As you progress through the guide you will discover that it contains many anecdotes from my own travels. These include some of my best and worst moments on the road in trying to bring Buddha nature to the problem at hand, and as often as not receiving an ironic and humbling lesson from the universe. Feel free to pass them by if you are in a time crunch or hear the conductor's call for the last train to the coast.

Let your life lightly dance
on the edges of Time
like dew on the tip of a leaf.

—RABINDRANATH TAGORE

1

The Method

Monkstown, Ireland, just outside of Dublin. May 21, 1994. I was six days into a shoestring vacation four years in the making and my day wasn't going that well. My back was hurting from an uncomfortable, overloaded pack; I had barely avoided a mugging after getting lost in the worst part of Dublin; and if I didn't get busy and find a suitable hotel I faced the prospect of scrambling around after dark and spending the night on a rubber bed in a cheap room populated by thoroughbred roaches. I had already pulled that trick three times since my arrival in London and I deserved better, especially tonight. It was the eve of my birthday.

> *You are a dynamic being of light that at each moment informs the energy that flows through you. You do this with each thought, with each intention.*
>
> *-GARY ZUKAV*

I scanned the main drag for a hotel and saw only one and it looked a little fancy. It surely boasted at least three stars, which meant it would violate my budget. I turned toward the other side of the street and spotted a quaint pub named O'Malley's, and the thought occurred to me that it was time for a break from my anxiety. A pint of Guinness would hit the spot and might be what I needed to revitalize myself and clarify my intentions. In a few minutes I was seated at the bar and waiting for the head to subside on a recently arrived pint.

The head was unusually frothy, as if agitated by some kind of atmospheric or ethereal disturbance—fairies perhaps—so to kill a few minutes, I removed pen and paper and began scrawling a letter home. Unbeknownst to me, the Buddha had taken the barstool next to me and was quaffing down my beer.

My pen skipped across the page as I described the recent events and my own hand in precipitating them. The confession would have impressed a Vatican priest. As I turned back to fortify myself with a swig of Guinness, I was overcome by a general feeling of well-being. Perhaps this was due to the simple act of discharging or maybe surrendering to the moment rather than worrying about the uncertainties that lay ahead. In any case, my back, which earlier had been creaking and aching, felt almost lithe; my spirit, previously dense as lead, seemed almost mercurial. It was good to be here and good to be alive, even though prospects for an affordable and restful night's sleep looked pretty bleak.

Six Irishmen trooped by me into a small ante-room, all of them smiling engagingly. They ordered beer and fell into good-natured banter. One of them raised a toast to Michael, "the birthday boy."

I turned and blurted out, "It's your birthday today? Mine is tomorrow. Can I buy you a pint?" The words had barely escaped my lips when the group invited me to join them. A few minutes later we were exchanging stories about mischievous fairies, singing rocks, and the magic of travel.

"You know you should join us at the party tonight," piped Seamus, the jolliest member of the group, who at five-foot-five with curly red locks, could have passed for a leprechaun.

"Yes," the others seconded.

I explained that nothing would please me more but that I needed to find a place to stay, then do laundry.

"We insist," declared a woman named Sheila. "We will celebrate Michael's birthday before midnight and yours after. And you won't need a place to stay. Someone will put you up."

I couldn't refuse.

After paying the tab I turned toward the door following Michael.

"Where are you headed?" he asked.

"Down south." I was actually headed for an international psychology conference in Killarney, but figured this would kill the conversation. After all, these people seemed pretty down-to-earth.

"Down south—Cork, Killarney?" asked Seamus.

"Killarney," I answered. "Going to a conference there." I wasn't going to be too specific.

"Oh, you mean the International Conference on Transpersonal Psychology, Ecology, and Spirituality. We're all headed there ourselves."

"You're kidding," I replied in shock.

"Oh, no. We're all counselors and physical therapists."

Was this possible? There couldn't be a dozen people in all of Ireland attending the conference and I had run into most of them here in a pub, 500 miles away on the eve of my birthday.

The party that night was more inspired and heartwarming than I could have imagined—full of eloquent toasts, joyful traditional dance, musical solos, and recitations. We sang; we danced; we shared ideas and outrageous stories. And the next day I headed south to Killarney for a conference that was equally rich with ideas and deep personal connections. I followed this up with a trip to the Continent where I was barraged with synchronicities and meaningful events that in one way or another linked back to O'Malley's.

The conclusion was inescapable that the events in the pub were not simply random. Clearly they flowed from the unexpected visit by the Buddha and my modest practice of mindfulness.

The Buddha taught that on everyone's path are a series of opportunities, hindrances, and obstacles that in some way reflect what is inside us. Inner and outer reality dance together, giving us a chance to affirm our own higher powers and break out of our conditioned responses, attachments, and self-limitations.

In some cases this simply requires breathing deeply and letting anxieties pass. In other cases, it requires taking stock of our surroundings, penetrating self-created distortions, asking ourselves—what is the big picture is here? What is the pattern that I am caught up in? What choices am I making that determine my day? What forces and energies are at work that I am pointlessly opposing?

Until my stop at O'Malley's I had been chasing my own tail, fighting and resisting every impediment, and losing track of choices I was making that were wearing me down spiritually and emotionally. After the visit by the invisible Guinness-guzzling Buddha, everything was different.

Beginning the next day (and on all subsequent trips) I traveled with a different vision and sensibility. My own personal Buddha was with me, like it or not, prodding me to see and make sense of the unfolding drama, and always urging me to consider how each experience reflected and projected what was inside me.

Travel I increasingly saw as an energized open-ended drama, with hidden plots and subplots about choices, mental frames, action, and inaction. The great challenge was to penetrate the scrim and see what was really going on, spiritually and emotionally, and how this shaped events and outcomes. Dealing with money problems, getting from one point to another, finding a room, or making personal connections were not simply about resources, planning, and organization, but about blind spots and their source, and above all, about equanimity. Travel was always a drama about inner balance.

The conscious act of self-monitoring produced amazing results, amazing opportunities—new friendships, exposure to new ideas, and joyful, often euphoric experiences that outstripped my imagination.

In my recent trips these have included the following:

1. *The development of long-lasting friendships in Ireland, France, Germany*
2. *An intimate relationship with a beautiful Bavarian woman*
3. *Business connections in London*
4. *A day at the races in Paris on which I could do no wrong*
5. *Inspiration for a novel which came quickly in the aftermath of my trip*
6. *Personal insights on the workings of grace, death, and dying*
7. *An invitation for a subsidized stay at an artistic retreat in Devon, England*
8. *Tutoring by an accomplished marine artist in Brittany*
9. *Meaningful and intimate conversations with prominent scientists, writers, and healers*
10. *A score of book references which led to leaps in my self-education*

In each case the gain transcended the immediate experience. Friendships were an affirmation of my ability to communicate with others from different cultures, speaking different languages. Creative breakthroughs in writing and painting affirmed the need to see differently in order to create with more power and expressiveness.

Every bit as edifying as the positive experiences have been the debacles and disasters. I've had more than a few. It often seems that my invisible, not-so-svelte travel companion takes as much delight in my mistakes and pratfalls as in my coups. All experience is simply raw material for more drama, however black, that leads to insights about Buddha nature, practiced and unpracticed. Among my award-winning stumbles and bumbles have been the following:

1. *Spending the night in the cold outside a Brienz hostel. (I was inadvertently locked out by the manager and spent a night outside in minimal clothing.)*
2. *Leaving behind my traveler's checks in the States on a trip to Europe in 1996. (I lived like a street person until I could get my family to wire me money.)*
3. *Catching the European grippe on a winter trip to London after the airline lost my luggage. (Picture a middle-aged man huddled in blankets in a freezing London hotel room. Buddha abandoned me to play darts at a nearby pub.)*

It was not always easy to discover the source and cause of each trauma. In each case I had to replay in my mind what had happened.

At the Brienz hostel the drama was about terrible time management, shame, and stoicism. I never would have been locked out if I hadn't returned to the hostel so late in the evening. I probably could have brought someone to the door if I had exercised my lungs but I couldn't bear the shame of that and remained silent. So with the temperature falling toward freezing, I retreated in shivers to a nearby village where I took refuge in a fire-station lavatory.

There a thunderbolt struck: I might be able to stave off hypothermia by stuffing my clothing with toilet paper. In a few minutes I looked like the Michelin Man, stuffed and puffed. Waddling back to the hostel, I began to warm up. I prostrated myself on a lawn next to the

Brienzer See (the lake next to the hostel) and stared motionlessly upward at the Swiss moon. The insulation was working perfectly. I was almost toasty when I lapsed into slumber. Little did I know that I had left a trail of toilet paper for a quarter mile back to the fire station.

Much later when I was on a train for Austria, the farce of this episode came to me and so, too, the fact that ego had authored this craziness. Pride and misguided aspiration to be self-reliant had kept me from rousting the manager. Apparently I would rather die of hypothermia than ask for anyone's help, especially if it meant calling attention to my own mistakes.

Paradoxically, the traveler's check debacle was about overpreparation. I had been so obsessed with preparing for my trip that I had succumbed to list-mania, that confused state of overpreparation in which the big picture pales. In packing I had let minutiae take over, worrying as much about a pencil sharpener as a passport, as much about my toenails as my traveler's checks. All at once I had been in a frenzy to make my flight, and in my haste I had left behind what mattered most.

"Travel light, especially light of mind," informed the Buddha. He might also have said, "If you live by the checklist, you also perish by it."

In the case of the London flu, the obvious lesson was about being penny-wise and pound-foolish—another form of myopia. I had refused to buy new clothes or spend the added amount for a hotel with central heating because I was more concerned about a future peril than a present one. This made no sense in light of the fact that my health was shaky even before I boarded my flight. There was no way I was going to avoid getting sick if I didn't keep myself warm.

The Clint Eastwood line comes to mind: "A man has got to know his limits." Obviously I didn't.

Buddhism teaches that difficulties such as these are often born from distortion, overreaction, compulsions, and ego attachments. Ego causes us to see the world the way we do and to make the choices that so often traumatize us. We choose to create our own check-lists and go over them in a particular way; we choose to yell or not to yell; we choose to huddle in the cold rather than spend our precious money.

The silent Buddha speaks when we have stilled our own noise and turbulence. If we are watchful and attentive we can see how the distortion occurred and how it was authored by ego. Taking on such personal responsibility is seldom easy. It usually requires swallowing pride. And yet it promises escape from the Mr. Magoo syndrome of myopically bouncing from one misadventure to the next with no apprehension of what is driving each event, thus causing us to experience the same basic problems in slightly different ways. The challenge is to take advantage of our inner acuity, to make it work for us in avoiding the cliff-drops and hidden minefields, and if we still can't escape them, endure them with grace.

The Essence of Mindful Travel—Find the Drama and Embrace It

In a thumbnail, each vacation may be viewed as a drama in which spirit, mind, and body are tested by impediment and opportunity. On the one hand, we are involved in outward exploration of unfamiliar geography, architecture, history, and foreign customs. In the process we must learn how to penetrate language barriers, decipher schedules, deal with lost luggage, orient ourselves in strange cities, and keep ourselves healthy under stress. On a more fundamental level, we are involved in a subtle inner drama that involves self-identity and personal meaning delivered through our response to impediments.

Almost always our impediments and obstacles are related to what is going on inside us. What is inside determines what we perceive, what we are drawn to, and what we avoid. Our inner struggle also accounts for our blind spots that play out dramatically in our choice of travel companions, decisions about health, and turns at each fork in the road.

What we think and what we are aware of also guide the experiences that come our way. This is the domain of the extended mind that reaches out to create synchronicities, uncanny human connections, and unpredictable opportunities. We have all experienced these but too often write them off as flukes. They aren't flukes but resonant grace notes from a charged consciousness.

This capacity to influence events through thought and observation has long been accepted by the great world religions. As stated in the Bible (John 3:8), we are body and soul but spirit is greater than our bodies and our souls. It blows where it will.

Divine grace and "the Holy Ghost" are kindred notions. Many Christian theologians view grace as a blessing that flows from spiritual connection to God. Prayer itself is often viewed as a two-way energetic communion that can invoke the Holy Spirit in a personal way.

Other religions and philosophies recognize the same link between inner and outer, between the act of reflection and what we experience on our individual paths. This concept is particularly strong in Judaism, Taoism, and Buddhism. Tibetan Vajrayana Buddhists are known to practice a special kind of visualization that purportedly results in materialized thought forms called *tulpas.*

Such practice is beyond me but all my trips seem to be affected by an ineffable intelligence. Herein lies the ultimate challenge in travel—perceiving and taking advantage of the visible and latent dramas that swirl around us and that are at least partially authored by our own projective powers.

It is hardly a new story. If you probe carefully you can find it in most of the epic myths—Perceval in seeking the grail, Ariadne in working her way through the labyrinth, and Odysseus in his travels through the Mediterranean. It is also reflected in the pilgrimages and journeys to enlightenment of sages and mystics. These include Buddha, Christ, Krishna, and Mohammed. In each case, the journey is only complete when the hero as humble "everyman" sheds his clumsy self-protection and armor and divests himself of ego. This is the process that allows Odysseus to find his way back to Ithaca, Perceval at last to pose the right questions to the Grail King, and Buddha to shake his confusion and discover a whiter light beneath the Bodhi tree.

The Power of Journal Keeping

Journal keeping can be the indispensable beam for illuminating a travel path. By keeping a daily log, you add discipline to your reflection and thereby raise the voltage and amperage on your insights. Unconscious motivations and impulses are clarified and you see what otherwise lay in shadows.

It is the rare person who can accomplish this through meditation alone. I am no exception. I need tools to focus my attention, and for me, no tool is quite so powerful in crystallizing clear thought than writing. As the writer and spiritualist Myra Zylstra has observed, "I'm often not sure what I think until I write it down."

I would go one step further—I'm often not sure what happened to me until I struggle to write it down. Journal keeping gives form and structure to gamboling thoughts and spinning impressions. The light metaphor again applies: insights are like nebulous waves of emergent consciousness bound up in a flux of charged impression. Journal keeping or writing collapses the flux. At once ideas, choices, and possibilities come to life that not only trigger insights but point you down another travel path toward people, places, and events that give meaning to what you do.

Steps for Mindful and Inspired Travel

The method is designed to promote useful reflection on travel experiences and to help the traveler harmonize these experiences with heartfelt intentions. It recognizes the many ways in which travel stresses can derail and sidetrack you, and it provides guidelines for regaining direction. It consists of ten basic steps that revolve around journal keeping.

Individual chapters guide you through the steps and provide tips for dealing with specific travel problems and contingencies. (The steps are listed in table 1–1.)

How This Method Differs
from Other Types of Journal Keeping

Travelers keep journals for different reasons and give them variable amounts of energy. Many are unadorned, minimal logs that record basic events, itemize and track expenditures, and record names and addresses of people encountered along the way. Others take a more literary bent, recording the sensory delights of experience, including meetings with people along the way.

This method allows for both but it focuses on what is happening internally to the traveler as he or she encounters opportunities and impediments, is frustrated and fulfilled, and goes through emotional highs and lows. It is designed to uncover the dramas, visible and hidden, in travel, and jog reflection on the spiritual experience. In the process you become both sleuth and navigator, uncovering insights that can enrich your trip as well as inform your daily life when you return home.

What Kind of Trips Can This Technique Be Used On?

The technique may be used on a variety of trips—for business or vacation, for reunions and pilgrimages. It applies just as well to tour and nontour travel, solo journeys and those with partners. It also lends itself to travel at different budget levels.

Most of my own vacation trips tend to be open-ended, inexpensive backpacking sorties, along the lines described in *Let's Go* (Harvard Student Agencies) or by Rick Steves in *Europe Through the Back Door*

(John Muir Publications). I usually buy a Eurail Pass and follow a flexible plan that centers around a few prearranged events (such as a conference in a foreign country or a meeting with someone I have contacted in advance). Most of these trips emphasize mobility and spontaneity and the challenges of traveling light. The method, however, can work just as well for someone traveling with a tighter itinerary or a higher budget, as well as for business travelers.

Used for business trips, the method can promote new relationships, partnerships, and product development. It facilitates the kind of reflection that calls out skills appropriate to the moment—discrimination and reason, communication skills, creativity and intuition—each of which may be beneficial depending upon the circumstance. On more than a few occasions I have used the mindful practices to redefine a business strategy or reformulate career goals and directions. The various practices have also sparked powerful synchronistic connections with future partners and helped me realize an important technical breakthrough.

Traveling with others on a vacation tour presents special challenges. One of the advantages of tour travel is that it allows you to devote yourself to priorities and leave the concerns of food, lodging, and transportation to others. The price you pay is limited choice, limited free time, and less privacy. For this reason the method only works on tours when you can separate yourself from the tour long enough to reflect on your experiences.

If this can be accomplished, take time to consider how your range of experiences is being prefigured by the way you are traveling. Ask yourself how the tour is limiting the range of people you meet and what you experience.

Materials Required

In order to practice this method you will need the following materials:

1. *A blank travel journal formatted as described in chapter 2. Ideally your book will be durable and compact.*
2. *Pencil and pen. If you plan to make drawings you may want to include color pencils, pastels, or other art materials.*
3. *Several durable Manila envelopes or large Ziploc bags that will serve as supplemental containers.*
4. *Envelopes, stamps, and stationery for letters.*

The time requirements for using the method will vary depending upon how fastidious you are and how experienced you are with the method. Here is my own time budget, which might be viewed as near-minimum requirements.

Table 1-1

Minimum Time Requirements for Using the Method

Step	Activity	Time Requirements	Which Chapter
1	Selecting and Buying the Journal	Minimal	Chapter 2
2	Formatting the Journal	15 minutes	Chapter 2
3	Defining Your Spiritual Touchstones	1 hour	Chapter 3
4	Self-Inventory	1 hour	Chapter 4
5	Identification of Intention and Objectives	$1/_2$ hour	Chapter 5
6	Identification of Travel Budget and Strategy	1 hour	Chapter 6
7	Daily Log and Monitoring	$1/_2$ hour/day	Chapter 7
8	Deeper Probing Chapters	1 hour/day (optional)	Chapter 7, 8
9	Troubleshooting and Rebalancing	2 hours/week	Chapter 9, 10
10	Debriefing	2 hours	Chapter 11

Who and Where Is the Buddha?

The danger of following any method or technique is that it may not fit perfectly with your own needs, and in following it you will shut down your creativity. For this reason you should only view the method as raw material for your own customized practice of mindful travel. Feel free to pick and choose elements and ideas; only take on what seems meaningful to you. Remember that *no one knows you as well as you,* and no one can better understand your needs than you.

This is an important if often overlooked element of Buddhism. As the psychologist Sheldon Kopp put it—"If you meet the Buddha on the road, kill him." Translation: find your own truth, disavow dogma and gurus. Siddhartha, the Gautama Buddha, needed to leave behind the Brahmin priests and their dogma in order to reach his own enlightenment. Breaking away is essential to self-discovery. We must all find our own path and create our own humble authority: *no gurus; no patriarchs in white robes; no authoritative preachers pronouncing dogma. Let them have their say; thank them for their input and concern; and send them packing.*

2
Getting Started with the Right Materials and Mindset

Most of my early trips were more akin to prison breaks than vacations. Whenever I had enough money and time for an extended trip to Europe I took it, which often meant I had little opportunity to plan and certainly little chance to think about the spiritual side of my trip. The last week before each flight would be a confusion of runs to the bank, the travel agent, and finally a bookstore where I would buy a travel guide, maps, and a notebook to record events, phone numbers, and expenditures. Journal keeping was an afterthought. Sometimes I would not even give it attention until I landed in London, Paris, Amsterdam, or Copenhagen.

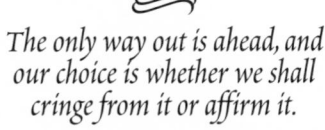

The only way out is ahead, and our choice is whether we shall cringe from it or affirm it.
    -ROLLO MAY

I came to discover the craziness of this. Travel mattered to me—it was as important as art, music, and writing, which I viewed as indispensable to my health and spiritual well-being. For these activities I always gave attention to preliminaries. I knew, for example, that good writing benefited from consideration of characters, plot, and themes. Paintings were more powerful if they began with some initial sketchwork.

I suppose my lack of forethought had something to do with my notions of freedom. A trip was always an expression of freedom, and maximum freedom was always the goal, which I equated with spontaneity and living in the moment. Unfortunately the closer my trips came to this ideal, the more unfree I seemed to be as I always wasted inordinate amounts of time troubleshooting and taking care of problems that could have been avoided. In Buddhist terms my trips and mindset were out of balance, suffering from "dukkha" (friction, static, and frustration) like an out-of-kilter wheel.

I decided to give more attention to preliminaries. The preparation, I realized, sets a tone and rhythm for what you will experience during your trip, and maybe most important, it initiates your mindfulness— the state of mind you may practice once your train arrives or your plane hits the tarmac. If your trip is launched in noise and static, if it begins in confusion and turbulence, this is probably what you will first experience, and maybe all that you experience.

Step 1. Selecting and Buying Your Journal

Since your journal will provide window and lens to your deeper self, invest in high-quality crystal—don't scrimp when it comes to purchasing a notebook and the other materials for journal keeping. Honor the process. Invest in quality binding, heavy paper, and a sturdy cover that will survive the elements and the stresses of travel. This will not only pay off in terms of durability but set a graceful tone for your reflection.

I used to buy a cheap college-lined notebook with spiral binding, in part because I wanted to travel light. I always paid a price for this.

Because I was backpacking I was constantly stuffing my journal in my day pack and before long it would look as though it had been quartered by bulldogs. It was never very long before dog ears appeared and the inside edges of the pages were shredded by the wire binding.

When it came time to record and reflect on my daily events, I couldn't see much point in being neat and careful, and this in turn affected my journal keeping. Often it consisted of illegible scribbles that recorded little more than the day's events and encounters. Insights seldom rose above candlepower, and I'm sure this affected my experiences on the road.

Since 1996 my journals have been durable sketchbooks, specially formatted, containing substantial paper, 40 lb. or heavier, suitable both for drawing and writing. I choose unlined sketchbooks because drawing is an important part of my reflection process and I don't like to carry one book for drawing and one for writing. The disadvantage of this is that writing without lines is sometimes difficult (especially for someone like me who would never make it as a Benedictine scribe). One compensating factor is that sketchbook paper and binding are often superior to writing books (although this seems to be changing). For me acid-neutral or acid-free paper is also worth the investment because I want my journals to last.

Whether you choose a sketchbook or lined notebook, make sure that the binding will hold up and that the book will lay flat when you are drawing or writing. (Books without spiral binding usually don't, and this can be frustrating, especially when you are drawing.)

A recent development is the spiral-bound notebook with hard cover. A number have come on the market with the increased interest in journal keeping. These are very durable but often lack blank pages, and perhaps more important, they are often formatted in ways that may not fit your needs. In general, I steer clear of any blank journal that contains sections which don't fit with my own recording and reflection process (see below for my own unique needs).

Assuming that you purchase a durable, high-quality journal, you may initially experience an aversion to cluttering it up with half-baked thoughts and drawings. Nip this in the bud. You aren't trying to produce a polished, unblemished work of art but to jog awareness. To accommodate working thoughts, reserve space in the back of your journal, maybe around 15 pages. If this isn't enough you can write on scraps of paper and store the surplus in Ziploc bags. (I find that using Ziploc bags is preferable to buying a notebook with pockets. The pockets invariably overflow.)

If at the end of your trip you wish to clean up some of the clutter and illegibility, allow yourself to prune and edit. In some cases I actually use an X-acto knife to remove cluttered, incoherent pages and transcribe the thoughts on unused pages.

The size and weight of your journal are also important. The volume should accommodate reflections, the recording of expenses, and permit unbounded brainstorming and expression, but unless you fashion yourself as an Edward Gibbon or James Michener spare yourself the burden of a book that could narrate the rise and fall of the Roman Empire.

Because each person and each trip are different, it is hard to satisfy everyone's needs with a single-size journal. However, length of the trip is a key factor. Correspondingly, I allow 200 pages for a six-week trip, 130 pages for four weeks, and at least 80 pages for trips of two weeks or less. This gives me at least four pages per day for daily entries, plus space for other important sections (approximately 40 pages).

Step 2. Organizing and Formatting Your Journal

By formatting my journal in advance, I can structure my reflection process to fit with the time limitations of travel. This pays dividends when you are running on empty late at night and don't feel much like reflecting and recording.

A recommended format is provided in table 2-1. There are five major sections separated by tabs. Within each section there are subsections labeled by headings. The estimated pages for each section are given in column 2 of the table.

Table 2-1
Suggested Format for Travel Journal

Journal Sections and Subsections	Number of Pages to Reserve in Journal
Section 1. General (Tab)	16
Headings:	
—Nameplate and return address	None
—Spiritual touchstones	2
—Intentions and objectives	2
—Strategy and budget	2
—Basic calendar (planned)	1
—Actual calendar	1
—Self-inventory barometers	1
—Buddha mandalas	2
—Expense summary by day	1
—Money exchanges	$1/_2$
—ATM withdrawals	$1/_2$
—Letter log	$1/_2$
—Photo log	$1/_2$
—Address book	2

Table 2-1
Suggested Format for Travel Journal

Journal Sections and Subsections	Number of Pages to Reserve in Journal
Section 2. Daily Log (Tab)	6 per day
Headings:	
—Daily expenses	$^1/_2$ per day
—Daily log of events, adventures, connections, thoughts	$4^1/_2$ per day
—Daily barometers of physical, emotional, spiritual condition	$^1/_2$ per day
—Mandala ratings of Buddhas at the wheel	$^1/_2$ per day
Section 3. End of Week or Periodic Review (Tab)	4 per review
Heading:	
—Themes, finances, ratings, progress	
Section 4. End of Trip Debriefing (Tab)	6
Headings:	
—Intentions and objectives realized	
—Dramas	
—Discoveries and insights	
—Capacities tapped/untapped	
—Unfinished business	
—Resolutions	

Section 5. Appendices (Tab)	30

Headings:

—Appendix 1: Brainstorms and creative products—	
sketches, theories, insights, letters	15
—Appendix 2: Working plans for trip, including maps	15

Supplementary Materials

   Manila envelopes or Ziploc bags labeled as follows:

1. Receipts

2. Money exchanges

3. ATM withdrawals

4. Address slips, names, references

5. Travel materials—past

6. Travel materials—prospective (including accommodations)

7. Letters (copies)

Use table 2–1 to guide your own formatting. You might want to attach tabs at the beginning of each section, as I do.

Formatting Your General Section

Spiritual Touchstones, Objectives, and Strategy for Your Trip

   Provide space at the front of your journal for your spiritual touchstones (discussed in chapter 3 below). Touchstones are your core beliefs and consist of a series of simple declarations (with or without justification). Two blank pages should suffice. Once you have finished chapter 3, you should be able to write them. The Intentions and Objectives section consists of a series of simple statements that describe what you want out of your trip. In the Strategy and Budget section you describe how you intend to reach your objectives and spend your time and money. At this point simply set aside the space in the front of your journal and provide headings.

Calendars

Your calendars are of two types: (1) a general or planned itinerary by day and date and (2) the *actual* place where you spent a given day or night. The purpose of including both is to facilitate comparisons between what you planned and what you experience so that you can reflect on the evolution of your trip and your mindset.

I use a grid format for my calendars and create them with a straight-edge.

m	t	w	th	f	sat	sun

Sample Calendar (Planned or Actual)

In each cell of my actual calendar I record the date, day of the week, my overnight location, and a simple highlight for the day.

Single Cell Blow-up of Actual Calendar

W	2/16
Louvre w/Bernadette	
Chantilly	

Create the blank calendars now, allocating space for each day of your travel week.

Barometers of Physical, Emotional, and Creative Condition (in General Section)

Your barometers are your personalized indexes for rating your physical, emotional, and creative condition. You will make these ratings on a daily basis, but in order to set up the process you will need to establish benchmarks. The benchmarks are your rating criteria. They define what it means for you to be doing well (or not so well) physically, spiritually, emotionally, and so on. I use a five-point scale as indicated below.

Physical Condition Barometer

#	Rating	Jim's Personal Benchmarks
5	Excellent	Energetic, no allergies, back OK, no diet problem, indigestion, no sniffles
4	Good	No problems but not optimal energy or digestion
3	Fair	Some allergies; back tight; throat tight
2	Poor	Labored breathing, back going out
1	Terrible	Sick, especially with respiratory problems

Emotional/Spiritual Condition Barometer

#	Rating	Jim's Personal Benchmarks
5	Excellent	In flow with synchronicities, joyful; Buddha nature in control; more life and experience!
4	Good	Curious, alive
3	Fair	Blowing hot and cold
2	Poor	Not exploratory; self-doubt erupting; sad; voices disabling me
1	Terrible	Ready for a leap off a high cliff; voice of limitation in control

Creative Condition Barometer

#	Rating	Jim's Personal Benchmarks
5	Excellent	Powerful writing or sketches; bursting with good ideas taken to higher level; co-creative conversation with others
4	Good	Good ideas sparking
3	Fair	Not much is happening but trying; taking in info, stimuli
2	Poor	No impulse to create; tired
1	Terrible	Empty as a dry river bed

Go ahead and create your barometers now and enter them in the front of your journal.

The Mandala

The mandala expresses aspects of Buddha nature that you would like to emphasize on your trip. On a daily basis I review them to assess

Mandala of Your Buddha Nature

Explorer

Enlightened
Warrior

Thinker

Communicator

Healer

Harlequin

Artist

Mystic

how I am doing and what I need to work on. At this point all you need do is to reserve space at the front of your journal (2 pages) and in your day section (1/2 page for each day). If you choose you can create the basic circles now but later you will need to decide on the inner contents (wedges of the pie). In chapter 4 I will guide you through this process.

Creating the mandalas freehand may be one of the most formidable tests of your Buddha nature (Buddha as Artist). Should you pass this test you obviously have no business mucking around on the earth

Table 2–2
Master Summary of Daily Expenditures

Date	Location	Total expenses	Other Currency	Lodging	Food	Big Ticket Items
2/20	France	$140	700ff	200ff/$40	100ff/$20	Train to Nice 200ff

plane and may go directly to Nirvana. In chapter 4, I will guide you through the process of creating mandalas.

Expenses and Accounting

Everyone has different accounting needs and different preferences for tracking expenditures. My convention is to create a master summary in my General Section, which gives category totals and carries forward the most important summary information from my daily accounting (see chapter 7). I use this for an overview of trends—to check expenses against budget. Above I show my summary table for a day in France when I traveled to Nice.

Note that amounts are standardized in dollars to facilitate daily comparisons. **Go ahead and create the master summary table now and enter it in your General Section.**

Money Exchanges, ATM Withdrawals, Credit Card Purchases

These tables should record where your important transactions occurred and how much money was involved. They should also note type of currency, fees, and transaction costs. For money exchanges I like to record exchange rates. **Go ahead and create the tables now and enter them in your General Section.**

Letter and Photo Logs

You may find it useful to maintain a simple record of letters written and sent during your trip. Something similar can be done for photos if photography is an important interest of yours. My letter log includes the date of each letter, the name of the recipient, the place where the letter was composed, and the general subject matter. On some trips I actually copy letters and store the copies in Ziploc bags, but this can add substantially to your burden.

Address Book

Although I usually bring along a small address book for home phone numbers and addresses and could use this to record new names and numbers, I like to create a unique listing of people I meet on the road. These new encounters give a unique signature to each trip and each journal. I reserve 2 pages in my journal for recording names, dates of meeting, phone numbers, and addresses (including e-mail addresses, of course). **Go ahead and create the table now and enter it in your General Section.**

Daily Log Formats

Be sure to leave enough room for daily entries (at least 5½ pages), which will include space for narratives (3 to 4 pages), mandalas, barometers, and itemization of expenses. See chapter 7 for elaboration on what you might record in your daily log.

3
Your Spiritual Touchstones

Y our spiritual touchstones are your core beliefs and provide bearing in moments of confusion, disorientation, and self-doubt. They may be likened to the lodestones of the great explorers that established magnetic north and offered a steady point of reference when the seas were roiling and the winds were driving *Ganymede, Santa Maria,* and the *Golden Hind* off course.

Since childhood I have been fascinated by the voyages of discovery and relished the dramas of exploration in *terra incognita,* particularly the way intrepid explorers escaped and survived man-eating lions, force-five gales, and rivers falling off the face of the earth.

> Each man must dig his own foundation
> -HENRY MILLER
>
> *It is the beginning of wisdom when you recognize that the best you can do is choose which rules you want to live by.*
> -WALLACE STEGNER

A favorite was the story of the Spaniard, Nuñez Cabeza de Vaca, who explored the American southwest in the 1500s, and set the standard for navigating into trouble. On an expedition through the wilds of Florida and Texas, his party was decimated by starvation and disease, then the remaining members enslaved by Native Americans. Nuñez recorded the dire events in his journal.

While captive he was ordered to heal a sick and dying tribal member. His dilemma was clear—refusal would mean his own death, and yet if he played doctor, the fellow would still die and it was obvious who would pay for that.

At a loss, he stepped forward, bowed in prayer, and offered a comforting hand and prayer. Somehow the tribesman recovered.

At once others begged for his help. Nuñez might have backed away and escaped while the halo over him was still intact, but chose instead to do what he could for the others. They too recovered spontaneously.

Although the story is enthralling and wondrous, its real power lies in the soul searching of Nuñez as he tries to make sense of what is happening. Each new healing provokes a probing of belief and humility and awe at the divine powers of the universe which he has somehow managed to tap. Shedding more and more ego, he draws closer to an inner radiance. His identity as *conquistador* falls away, replaced by that of compassionate mystic and healer. In the process he repeats the transcendent journey of Buddha on his way to the Bodhi Tree, Moses to the Mount, and Christ to the cross. Thus he arrives at the heart of his own Buddha or Christ nature.

Step 3. Defining Your Spiritual Touchstones

Touchstones are simple expressions of your fundamental spiritual values and beliefs. They capture important aspects of higher self-identity and faith.

Let us hope that you as traveler won't experience the travails of Nuñez, but if you are visited by the Four Horsemen of the Apocalypse, your touchstones can provide valuable direction and grounding. On more than a few occasions my own have given me a shot of energy when I was sure that Buddha nature had fled.

I like to begin every trip by recording my touchstones in the first few pages of my journal. This way I pass through them on my way to the daily log. In the process I get a reminder of who I am and what I believe in.

Each touchstone should be as brief and succinct as possible. Don't agonize in providing a rationale or justification (unless you want to). Whatever your reasons, they are sure to be valid.

Because people sometimes find it difficult to express core beliefs, I have included a few of my own to get your wheels turning. Below are the touchstones I recorded prior to a six-week trip to Europe. I have included elaboration so that you may understand how they speak to me and why.

Touchstone 1
The Traveler as Spiritual Being
〜

I am more than my physical body—a spiritual being with energetic capacities that transcend the physical plane.

Hindu mystics commonly speak of five different bodies that reflect spirit and life-force: the physical body, the etheric, the rational, the magical, and the spiritual. Each defines us as a unique body/mind/spirit. Our higher self is nonphysical and is referred to as Atman, however, it is inseparable from a collective God-force call Brahman. Tibetan Buddhism also asserts an imperishable *heart essence* that we take with us to the afterlife and potentially to subsequent lives. Both Judaism and Christianity also recognize a spirit or soul that transcends the physical body.

During travel it is important to affirm that we are more than the limited body that is being victimized by nasty train conductors, frisked and violated by overzealous customs officials, squashed by condescending hotelkeepers. Spirit survives and endures all slings and arrows, and it grows to the degree that we can get through each challenge without cursing the darkness or abusing others or ourselves for our failings.

Touchstone 2
Risk Is Indispensable to Discovery and Breakthrough

Remember that most of the great voyages of discovery involved leaps of faith by mariners sailing into uncharted seas toward new worlds. (Of course, a lesser number were unmitigated disasters led by a deluded Don Quixote sailing blithely off the face of the earth.) A check on who is at the wheel is clearly a good idea, but so, too, an objective view of whether you are holding on too tightly to what is known and familiar.

Henry Miller wrote, "Whatever there be of progress in life comes not through adaptation but through daring, through obeying the blind urge . . . The whole logic of the universe is contained in daring, in creating from the flimsiest, slenderest support."

The most courageous risk-taking has little to do with gambling or mountain climbing, adventures into darkest Africa or solo sailing expeditions. It is less about clinging to a vertical rock face than letting go of protection. Almost always this feels like shedding—divesting ourselves of ego, of concerns about what others may think or how we may be perceived. We stand naked in the affirmation of a higher self that may be rejected by others. In the process we open ourselves up to a more expansive, wider-ranging divinity.

If this is the kind of risk-taking that underlies and accompanies our treks to the Congo, sailing expeditions around Cape Horn, or assaults on Everest, then the risk is imbued with soulfulness and may be worth taking. The same can be said of simpler, less grandiose acts that go unnoticed or unpraised. For you the risk may be reaching out to a street person in New York or Calcutta, or breaking through your self-consciousness to communicate with a stranger. It may be the simple act of setting out on your own with a backpack, quelling worries about limited funds or the apprehensions about traveling solo on the road and rails.

Know that risk is in the eyes of the beholder, and that an inner Buddha appreciates our courage in the face of the uncertain. He or she will be there with you to surmount obstacles and impediments and practice grace through trauma and trial.

Touchstone 3
Expect the Unexpected and
Don't Sweat the Small Stuff
〜

Distant travel presents us with more uncertainties, glitches, and potential snafus than we can ever fully prepare for. Once we venture forth into unfamiliar territory we are bound to run into problems making connections, finding accommodations, changing money, and communicating with locals who have no clue

"Maybe I should have taken care of this problem before we shoved off."

what we are talking about. Sometimes our traumas are a result of customs and conventions that we don't fully understand, sometimes a result of people having a bad day and finding us to be convenient targets. If you personalize such noise and friction, you only drain your own energy, so shrug and shed it.

A good portion of the time, we blow such irritations out of proportion because of fatigue or poor health. To prevent this, do your best to stay rested and strong and nurture your spirit. The problem of staying strong may be likened to the problem of maintaining an old wooden boat. It will need to be caulked and painted if you are going to prevent major leaks and if you expect it to hold up in turbulent seas. If you put in the advance effort, you won't be devoting all your energy to bailing and hailing rescuers when the gales arrive.

Routine maintenance should include attention to diet and rest. Fortify yourself with quality toxin-free food and pure water. If your energy is low, spring for a night in a decent hotel. A night on a good mattress can do wonders.

Nurturing should include attention to spirit. Know what supports your Buddha nature and give it to yourself when you sense a loss of balance. For some people it is music that soothes the wobbling spirit; for others writing, art, or possibly random acts of kindness do this.

<table>
<tr><td>

Touchstone 4
Be Aware
of Ego Projections

</td><td>

Whenever we feel insecure or fearful, shadow impulses surface to protect imperiled ego. Negative voices tell us

</td></tr>
</table>

that the world is limited and dangerous; shortage abounds; and we are soon to be on the street, pushing shopping carts full of old shoes and newspapers. Besides leading a chorus on shortage, danger, and

Mindfulness precipitates a downpour of opportunity.

limitation, the shadow is the master of blame and finger-pointing, shaming, pontificating— all intended to prop up fearful ego.

This, in turn, engenders similar behavior from others: like begets like. Before long, trivial frictions turn into abuse and conflict that only hurt everyone involved.

By understanding shadow and making a commitment to transcend it, we release magical potential in ourselves and others. On some occasions the result is a field-like effect in which good fortune and opportunities abound. (I like to refer to this as "making the Buddha dance.")

Touchstone 5
Practice Meditation
and Self-Reflection
⁓

If I make sense of me, the patterns around me
will be become clear.

Trying to get from place to place on schedule and to satisfy basic needs, we invariably run into complications that heighten stress and cause our inner compass to spin out of control. Meditation silences the noise and turbulence and allows us to find our true bearings. First and foremost it creates space. In the emptiness that lies between thoughts, Buddha nature begins to stir and inform us of what we need to make ourselves whole or realize heartfelt intention.

A variety of simple meditative techniques are available that can help (see chapter 10). My own approach is to spend at least some time in the morning and evening in a quiet state, suppressing inner chatter, and practicing *prana* breathing.

⁓
To a mind that is still, the whole
universe surrenders.
-CHUANG TZU

Secretly we spoke, that wise one
and me. I said, "Tell me the
secrets of the world." He said,
"Sssh, let silence tell you the
secrets of the world."
-RUMI

⁓

A necessary complement to meditation is self-reflection. It tends to work best after we have stilled anxiety (for example, through meditation) and can look objectively at ourselves and what is disabling us. Once you have turned off the inner noise and chatter, play back the tapes of recent events, reviewing your role in creating them. What choices did I make? What skills and capacities did I use or not use that would allow me to practice Buddha nature? (See touchstones 3, 4, and 6.)

Touchstone 6
Inventory Who Is at the Wheel
↜

Remember that the Buddhas are standing by patiently, awaiting a worthy mission.

Within each of us are divine capacities to perceive, create, invent, communicate, adapt, and self-heal. These are reflected in eight archetypes, which may be viewed as incarnations of Buddha nature. Each archetype is defined by a particular mindset or orientation that brings special skills to problem solving. Buddha as Artist sees impediments in an artistic light and responds to creative challenges. Harlequin is performance and drama-oriented, while Mystic views reality through a spiritual lens and sees impediment as opportunity to realize deeper personal meaning.

Each mindset can be tapped to enrich experiences on the road. For example, Buddha as Mystic was the first to visit me at O'Malley's, causing my disarmed reflection on what had been happening to me. For the insight to surface I only needed to quiet myself, mute the hustle-bustle of the street, and reflect without ego on recent events. Buddhists refer to this as *invoking the silent witness.*

Table 3–1
Incarnations of Buddha Nature

Archetype	Specialty
Artist	Master of Creative Expression
Harlequin	Master of Drama and Laughter
Communicator	Master of Language and Communication
Mystic	Master of Higher Consciousness
Healer	Master of Wellness
Enlightened Warrior	Master of Physical Discipline and Sacrifice
Thinker	Master of Critical Thinking and Reason
Explorer	Master of Resourcefulness

Writing brought out further insights as I gave myself up to Buddha as Harlequin, master of drama, who penetrated my self-created theater and how it was directing me. I could see both farce and tragedy and a not-very-pretty picture of future events if I didn't make some changes.

Then the Irish troupe caught my attention and Harlequin gave way to Buddha as Communicator. I put myself out to Michael and his friends, and they returned my openness and energy with an invitation to their birthday party. Later that night, Buddha as Harlequin again took to the stage, shamelessly performing an Irish jig, raising a semi-eloquent toast to the fairies, then telling a bald-faced-lie-of-a-story to a group of inebriated, sense-dulled therapists.

I provide a detailed account of the various archetypes in chapter 4.

> ## Touchstone 7
> ## Realize That You Are Not Alone
>
> ⌒
>
> *Individual mind is enfolded within a greater collective*
> *mind which can be tapped by transcending ego*
> *and shadow.*

Buddhism and Hinduism and various mystical traditions recognize the existence of a collective mind that we are all a part of. It is the repository of archetypes—good and bad—and accumulated human knowledge. It is also the field of higher possibility, including pure creativity and the physical laws that govern matter and energy.

Hinduism speaks of this collective mind as Brahman, which is marked by progressively higher states of consciousness that are accessible through spiritual practice. Buddhism contains similar ideas and emphasizes the attainment of insight by leaving behind earthly attachments, transcending ego, and becoming witness to the events that swirl around us.

Carl Jung gave a scientific basis to this notion of collective mind in his theory of the collective unconscious. He believed that as individuals we all belong to larger wholes. These wholes are held together by shared instincts, symbolic attractions, and myths. The collective unconscious not only stores memory but perpetuates it through ingrained behavior.

When traveling solo far from home, it is easy to surrender to feelings of loneliness or isolation. Distant from friends and family, we can easily feel separated and marooned. The rudeness or insensitivity of others can amplify our estrangement.

In such situations it is easy to forget the larger "family" that we never really leave behind. It is easy to forget that we are joined to others past and present in ways we don't fully comprehend. With mindfulness we can reach out to them and draw upon their supportive energies.

This is the experience I had in Ireland when I met Sheila, Michael, Seamus, and the others. Despite the fact that they lived in Dublin and I in Seattle, we were kindred spirits, committed to many of the same notions of service and self-awareness, and equally curious about the strange and often ironic workings of the mind. My connection with them was a powerful affirmation of a larger spiritual collective.

Touchstone 8
Recognize That Every Choice and
Action Engenders Consequences.
 ✑

Act with conscience and compassion

Compassion, generosity, love, and openness tend to return to those who practice them. Similarly, shadow behavior begets negativity from others. This is often called Karma. By being mindful of your thoughts and behavior you can often ameliorate the traumas you may be experiencing. "Give and you shall receive" is the rough equivalent in the Christian canon.

The notion of Karma is frequently distorted to explain away our foibles and debacles. Cliff-falls, train wrecks, and implosions of relationships are often ascribed to predetermination or destiny that can't be escaped—the individual is little more than a pawn or cipher, playing out scripted destiny. We only have real power to grin and bear it and comfort ourselves in the belief that perhaps the next time around our Karma will make life easier.

This is a convenient half-truth. Karma works both ways—from

outer to inner and inner to outer; from mind to life experience and back again.

The Karma I believe in, and the Karma that speaks to me in Buddhism, is also about personal responsibility and the choices we make to affect our lives and our environment during our limited stay on the earth plane. It is true that some of the important parameters are fixed. Others, I believe, are created by the society we live in and are visited upon us probabilistically. As near as I can tell, we have no say in our birth or the conditions surrounding it, including our nationality, race, birth family, and so on. Our death is also fated and we carry some constraints based upon our DNA, but much of our travel itinerary is plastic and affected by choice and decision.

Some amount of suffering is unavoidable—this is the human condition—but this does not mean that we play no role in it. As often as not we contribute to our worst debacles through lack of forethought, lack of attention, lack of mindfulness, overreaction, and the full range of our ego defenses.

Think of each situation in terms of a drama in which you are the protagonist. Ask yourself, how did I affect the outcome? Just by asking the question you are halfway to discovering the answer. And rest assured it will have little to do with destiny, fate, or a divine wish. The real Karma is about dynamics that are set in motion by the way we treat others and ourselves, and by our invocation or failure to call forth the Buddha within.

> *If we want to lead a creative life it is absolutely just that we should be responsible for our own destiny.*
>
> -HENRY MILLER

<table>
<tr><td>

Touchstone 9
Stay Tuned to the Drama and How
It Is Created

〜

</td><td>

As a species we are born to drama and the dramatic imperative is to discover our capacity to love, create, heal

</td></tr>
</table>

ourselves, help others, and protect the earth. Seeing and scripting drama is the domain of Buddha as Harlequin, the consummate actor, lover of theater, and the ham taking center stage.

Harlequin, playing out voices of limitation, is the bad actor caught up in a tired script. Without commitment to self-understanding, his roles are usually projections of shadow and self-limitation. The dramas he plays out are often trite and fear-based. Women are commonly caught up in Cinderella Complexes and men imitate Stallone or Schwarzenegger, fantasizing a false masculinity that has little to do with authentic power. There are countless variations on the theme as we try to satisfy aching needs for love, power, and acceptance.

For all the energy we devote to our distorted dramas, we could achieve more. When we escape the bad scripts and play out something more than shadow and ego, we give ourselves up to Harlequin, the master performer. At his best he outshines Burton and Brando, eclipses Shirley MacLaine and Elizabeth Taylor. Even the front row Buddhas applaud his performance, clapping wildly in unison (with one hand, of course).

Composing and Recording Touchstones

If my touchstones are not enough to help you define your own, you might perform a review of your most formative dramas, travel and otherwise. Ask yourself what experiences defined you as a person. In each case what core lessons were learned? What insights did you realize

"Isle of Pegasus" by Jim Currie.
A place for reflection and meditation.

about the power of prayer, helping others, about creativity or inspiration? Try to go beyond the surface notions to beliefs about higher self—what you aspire to in your most selfless moments. And then ask what forces of the universe you can draw on for support and what practices promote this.

A useful technique for crystallizing values is to imagine yourself on a high platform looking out on your own sacred world. (I transport myself to a place I call "the Isle of Pegasus." This is represented in my drawing of the same title.) Ask yourself: What is meaningful in my environment? What is precious and what is generative? What metaphysical forces can be tapped to sustain and support your mindfulness?

When you have completed your touchstones record them in the space you have provided in the General Section of your journal.

4
Self-Inventory: Getting to Know Your Buddha Nature

*B*uddha nature is your capacity to realize divine self. The purpose of your self-inventory is to sensitize yourself to different mindsets, or aspects of Buddha nature, which you may call upon when faced by impediment or opportunity on your travel path.

Obstacles and impediments are unavoidable in travel and are bound to create stress and duress, potentially causing the wheels to come off of a trip that might have been full of adventure, inspiration, and opportunity. Sometimes we aren't aware that we are reeling until it is too late. When I turned into O'Malley's on my trip to Ireland, I was fortunate enough to realize that something was out of round. Using the metaphor of the Buddha, I was ready to shine a lamp on myself in order to find out what was lacking and why. I might have done this earlier if I had been more aware of my own shadow and how it was doing me in.

> *He who knows himself, knows God.*
> *-AUGUSTINE*
>
> *Be lamps unto yourselves.*
> *-GAUTAMA BUDDHA*

Step 4. Self-Inventory: Define Your Buddha Nature

Choosing the right lamp and focusing the beam for maximum illumination is always a challenge. Monks commit their entire lives to reaching higher states of consciousness, and patients undergoing psychotherapy may be treated for a decade or more before they manage a breakthrough.

Short of a stay in a Lhasa monastery or extended counseling from a Viennese psychotherapist, you might consider a simple method I use in my own travels. It requires a simple pretrip inventory of the mindset you bring to different kinds of daily problems. This can help you clarify travel intentions and later, when you are on the road, facilitate your reflection and journal keeping.

The method includes five basic steps (4a to 4e).

Basic Steps in Defining Your Buddha Nature

4a. *Lineup of the Buddhas*
Review the aspects of your Buddha nature and mindsets appropriate for different kinds of problem solving.

4b. *Create a Mandala of Your Buddha Nature*
Characterize your own dominant Buddha nature and specify the Buddhas you invoke to deal with problems and situations at home and on the road.

4c. *Identify Shadow Voices of Limitation*
Examine the common voices of limitation that contract and stifle your Buddha nature. I describe some of the most common voices.

4d. *Relate Voices of Limitation to Buddha Nature*

Probe more closely the workings of the shadow. This includes looking at the relationship between strengths and weaknesses. Shadow behavior is often the result of taking strengths to excess or extreme. You are given examples of how this works in travel.

4e. *Create a Mandala Showing the Buddha Nature You Will Practice on Your Trip*

Identify the mindsets you need to work on most and the ones you will emphasize on your trip. You may link these to particular situations you expect to encounter on your trip.

You might ask whether such reflection might take the joy and spontaneity out of a trip. Valid question. None of us wants to be so much in our head that we can't experience the excitement of travel. But that isn't what is being suggested here. The self-inventory needn't take a great deal of time—only about an hour. Second, when you are on the road reviewing mindset, you aren't continuously taking stock, only performing a quick review at the end of each day. Finally, it is my experience that the joy and spontaneity of travel increases when choices, thought, and action are aligned with your higher self-identity, and that's what this can promote.

4a. Lineup of the Buddhas

Below I have sketched out some of the heartiest incarnations of Buddha nature. These aren't all-inclusive, only the ones that speak to me most powerfully during my travel. Feel free to add or subtract aspects of each archetype. In other words, review critically the credo and mindset of each Buddha and the questions and skills they bring to travel. Also, consider adding other Buddhas that you think are missing from my list but belong on yours.

Artist: Master of Creative Expression

Practices novelty, intuition, and visual expression and delights in spontaneity. Buddha as Artist disdains convention and conformity, always juggling and rearranging to create more powerful and resonant images.

Special Travel Skills of Buddha as Artist
    —depicting graphically a given problem or puzzle
    —juggling pieces of a puzzle for new perspective or insight
    —finding something novel and useful in the most dire occurrence
    —twisting reality to reveal a precious truth
    —creating art that expresses joy or captures emotion
    —turning shortage or setback into an artistic challenge

Mischievous Tricks and Modus Operandi
    —floating glass balls down the Grand Canal in Venice
    —creating and selling your own unique currency to keep a trip alive
    —producing a sidewalk drawing in chalk on Boulevard Montparnasse

Credo and Mindset	Special Questions and Curiosities
Avoid the beaten path.	How might I juggle the pieces of this situation to gain a clear insight?
Give me a pencil or crayon and I can illustrate and clarify the problems I am confronting.	How might I represent this problem or drama graphically to clarify it?
Materials abound to fuel my artwork.	What is the camouflage?
I have no trouble imagining an elephant dancing on the head of pin.	What is figure and what is ground?
The greatest masterpieces are still uncreated.	Where is the novelty in this experience?
Worry not about what is acceptable.	How do I prick this swollen bubble of ego and tired convention?

Harlequin/Jester:
Master of Drama and Laughter

Ably perceives abounding dramas; delights in performances; skilled role player and empath.

Special Travel Skills of Buddha as Harlequin
> —seeing humor in the foibles and frustrations of travel
> —laughing at the paradoxes and ironies encountered along the way
> —reading the underlying and hidden dramas of travel
> —imagining the plight of another
> —reading the behavior of others and how it might affect your trip

Mischievous Tricks and Modus Operandi
> —enjoying improvisation
> —reveling in the unpredictable
> —attempting to make the guards "crack" at Buckingham Palace
> —performing an impersonation when a crowd is gathered
> —looking for Robin Williams, Jim Carey, and other playmates

Credo and Mindset	Special Questions and Curiosities
I am the protagonist in my own drama to create.	What are the hidden dramas and conflicts?
If the drama eludes me, I need only shift my point of view.	What are the dynamics that are driving this drama?
For all your woes, I give you laughter.	What is the irony in this scene?
	What discarded banana peels may cause an unexpected slip-up?
I can empathize with others and take on their point of view.	How do I twist reality to provoke an insight?
There has to be a graceful solution to this mess.	How can I play this part with greater power?
	What would I see and feel if I were in someone else's shoes?

Communicator:
Master of Language and Communication

Skilled listener, attentive to different perspectives and mindsets; delights in bringing people together, promoting understanding and cooperation.

Special Skills of Buddha as Communicator
—being attentive to wishes and expression of others
—reading nonverbal communication and the emotion behind words
—showing compassion and concern for others
—reading the feelings and thoughts of travel companions
—negotiating with hucksters and making a good deal
—getting warring parties to bury their swords

Mischievous Tricks and Modus Operandi
—"all ears" for a good story
—dickering with used-car dealers and Turkish rug merchants
—speaking the local language whenever possible

Credo and Mindset	Special Questions and Curiosities
I can find the apt phrase or *mot juste* to describe a problem or situation.	What is being said without words?
	What is our common vocabulary?
I can cut through language barriers.	What meaning lies beneath the surface?
I can express and communicate the emotion behind different points of view.	Who is listening to whom and who is not?
I can find commonalties.	What hidden messages need to be brought to the surface?
I can mediate any dispute.	What are the sources of misunderstanding here?
I can disarm antagonists and get them to talk to one another.	How can we cut to the real issues?
	What are the possibilities for cooperation?

Explorer: Master of Resourcefulness

Ace inventor and improviser; delights in the challenges of limited resources and finding his way out of a dark forest.

Special Travel Skills of Buddha as Explorer
—leading a diverse group
—reading maps and getting oriented in strange surroundings
—jerry-rigging tools and instruments
—recognizing impediments and wasted energy
—avoiding a likely traffic jam
—putting the right person on the job and recognizing the talents of others

Mischievous Tricks and Modus Operandi
—using toilet paper as an insulator
—keeping a car running when it ought to be dead
—always on the lookout for a promising shortcut

Credo and Mindset	Special Questions and Curiosities
Obstacles and impediments are only a test of my resourcefulness.	What are the perils and opportunities on this landscape?
	Where are the shortcuts?
I am prepared to alter course to avoid obstruction.	What other tacks might prove more useful and productive?
I am attuned to the currents and landscape of my environment.	What preparation is in order for this voyage?
I can harmonize the energies and efforts of my crew.	What risks need to be taken and which avoided?
Give me some duct tape, wire, and a computer chip and I can create anything.	What tools would make this mission easier?

Mystic: Master of Higher Consciousness

Able to quiet chaos, transcend ego, and tap extended mind to help others and realize spiritual wholeness.

Special Travel Skills of Buddha as Mystic
　　—clarifying intention
　　—finding the relationship between events and higher purpose
　　—prompting synchronicities
　　—discovering higher insights
　　—reading the need for reflection and meditation
　　—reading the way mind toxins (such as addictions and attachments) are affecting travel

Mischievous Tricks and Modus Operandi
　　—reveling in synchronicities
　　—being on the lookout for instructive symbols, ironies
　　—enjoying the challenge of remaining calm and centered on a New Delhi train
　　—displaying telekinetic or other extrasensory powers
　　—offering a grin or smile to a cop after being ticketed
　　—calming and quieting barking dogs
　　—communicating love and compassion with attentiveness

Credo and Mindset	Special Questions and Curiosities
I can transcend ego.	What are my blind spots?
I can realize my higher self.	What are the higher-level questions?
I can quell my negative internal chatter through reflection, meditation, and mindfulness.	What are my voices of limitation and how do I transcend them?
I am more than my body, more than what I do, more than what I create, and more than what I think.	In what ways can I be of service to others?
I can be of service to others.	In what ways am I connected to others?
I can find joy in being, discovery, expression, and service.	Where is the path with heart?
Overboard with the baggage.	
I am grateful.	

Healer: Master of Wellness

Attuned to the ways in which mind interacts with body to create health or disable it; committed to helping others realize health and wholeness.

Special Travel Skills of Buddha as Healer
—recognizing unhealthy stress
—reading a weakened immune system
—boosting nutrition and overall wellness—staying warm, rested, and well nourished
—nurturing others who may be sick or in need of support
—knowing when a doctor should be called in for help
—getting rid of toxins or avoiding them

Mischievous Tricks and Modus Operandi
—recovering quickly from a cold that could have turned into the flu
—making practical suggestions to someone looking for help
—balking at drinking cola and other pop, instead using them as windshield bug-remover

Credo and Mindset	Special Questions and Curiosities
I can monitor my own health and detect imbalances before they surface in illness.	How is my mind/body system operating?
I can make changes to boost my immune system and attend to the root causes of illness.	What are the pathways by which imbalances manifest themselves in disease?
In order to heal others I may have to heal myself.	What are my personal weaknesses and vulnerabilities?
Caring, love, and compassion promote wellness and healing.	What signs and signals can I rely on to monitor my own health and wellness?
I can find the right people to help me answer the questions that are beyond my knowledge.	How am I affected by fatigue, depression, diet, flagging spirit?
	How can I fortify myself?
	What problems are beyond me and require help from others?
	How can I support and help others?

Enlightened Warrior:
Master of Physical Discipline and Sacrifice

Paragon of honor and integrity, skilled in reading forces on a battlefield and disarming aggressive destroyers.

Special Travel Skills of Buddha as Enlightened Warrior
  —dealing with fatigue late in the day while traveling
  —dealing with disorientation, discomforts in a foreign city
  —saying no to people or situations that are unhealthy
  —controlling negative emotions
  —helping those who are weaker in body or spirit
  —recognizing a path with honor and integrity and taking it
  —turning negative energy into positive energy

Mischievous Tricks and Modus Operandi
  —asking "Grasshopper" to "snatch the pebble from my hand"
  —reveling in the challenge of "redirecting chi"
  —traveling light physically and emotionally
  —slipping away from or flanking an aggressor
  —blending in with surroundings
  —smiling back at an enraged driver
  —staying composed in an overfull airliner

Credo and Mindset	Special Questions and Curiosities
Through will, discipline, and integrity I will surmount this problem.	How can I use the energy of my adversaries to bring peace and balance to this situation?
I can read the landscape ahead of me and prepare myself for conflicts that lay ahead.	What strength can I call on to get me through this?
I take responsibilities for my own difficulties.	What is the path of least resistance?
No need to pay for the same ground twice.	What contingencies should I plan for?
Always vigilant.	Who are my potential allies?
Semper fi.	How do I resolve this conflict without violence?
No need to get even, only stay in balance.	What is the path with honor and integrity?

Thinker:
Master of Critical Thinking and Reason

Ace problem solver and practitioner of logic, attuned to patterns, anomalies, and uncertainty.

Special Travel Skills of Thinker
—reading uncertainties and probabilities of different travel routes
—putting together timetables, rail and plane connections
—getting to the heart of a problem with a travelmate
—developing a workable plan or strategy
—finding the low-cost solution to any problem

Mischievous Tricks and Modus Operandi
—embracing the unsolved puzzle
—skillfully turning assumptions upside down to gain new
    perspective
—delighting in Occam's Razor—the simplest solution to a complex
    problem
—concocting a defining test or experiment

Credo and Mindset	Special Questions and Curiosities
I can work through this problem, using my life experience, training, education, and intuition.	What are the elements of the problem and how do they work together?
	What tools do I need to inform my choices?
At the heart of all problems are testable assumptions and propositions.	
	What are the competing hypotheses, solutions?
I can pose the right questions and hypotheses to clarify what is going on.	What evidence supports which solutions?
I can construct informative experiments and logical tests.	What are the uncertainties and how can I account for them?
	What tests can I use to confirm or validate a possibility?

4b. Create a Mandala of Your Buddha Nature

Now that you have reviewed different aspects of Buddha nature, create a mandala showing the mindsets you bring to daily problem-solving. (You will use this for Step 4e.) To complete the step, draw a large mandala divided into wedges that represent the different archetypes described in Step 4a. Within each wedge note specific ways you practice that aspect of Buddha nature.

Consider how you approach your job, how you deal with relationships, family, finance, hobbies, and property maintenance. Consider how much you emphasize will, intuition, creative or artistic insight, logic and rationality in different situations. If you bring more than one perspective (or archetypal mindset) to a class of problems, note the same problem in different wedges of the mandala. You needn't be exhaustive in this review as the point here is to promote awareness of your own *modus operandi* in different situations.

You are apt to discover that you practice dominant tendencies. For example, a great many creative people don't embrace the need to sell their ideas to others by using their marketing and communication skills. As a result, their ideas don't get off the ground. Likewise, some people rely heavily on reason and logic (Thinker) in giving counsel to friends when compassion and empathy (aspects of Communicator, Harlequin, Mystic, and Healer mindsets) might be more appropriate. Excesses are discussed more fully in Step 4d.

Mandala of Your Buddha Nature

4c. Identify Shadow Voices of Limitation

Voices of limitation erupt when we are insecure and feel imperiled by people and circumstances around us. In the process we stifle the various Buddhas. Energy which might have been devoted to creative problem-solving is used destructively to keep ourselves stuck.

When we take on a siege or victim mentality, we also engender anxiety, peril, and panic in others. They begin to see us in the same way we see them. Before long all the Buddhas (theirs and ours) have absconded, leaving us to our scapegoating, judgment, and recrimination.

A secondary effect of shadow behavior is that because we are contracted, we disconnect from higher collective-consciousness. The links we might have made to an extended super-mind are lost. Emotionally and creatively we are floating in space. When this occurs don't count on any thunderbolts from God about the great unwritten novel; don't expect that your hand will be guided to paint a Mona Lisa. And if you would like to make a connection with a smiling mademoiselle in the Paris Metro, brace yourself to be arrested for lewdness and assault.

Some of these toxic voices of limitation are presented in table 4-1.

4d. Relate Voices of Limitation to Buddha Nature

Quite often voices of limitation are perceived and rationalized as high-minded, honorable, and pure of heart when they are really fearful and anxious. For example, Buddha as Enlightened Warrior is a master of discipline, but under ego attack often turns into a flaming Ninja *destroyer*, lashing out at those around him using will and strength to overpower adversaries. We all have our rationalizations—others are malevolent and need to be stopped; others are guilty and misguided. This is shadow behavior and usually revealed by lack of compassion and forbearance. A *destroyer* mentality—although often directed at others—is usually self-abusive. Others may be blamed or faulted, but invariably the destroyer is saying something about his own perceived inadequacies and pain and usually finding a way to further wound himself in the process.

This relationship between shadow and Buddha nature is true of other Buddha incarnations, including Artist, Healer, Explorer, and so on. In effect, strengths taken to extreme become weaknesses.*

One of the reasons that these excesses occur is that we become habituated to responding to a problem in a particular way. We rely upon our familiar solutions and familiar responses, ignoring approaches that we are unaccustomed to. Then when the problem doesn't go away we reach for the twelve-pound hammer when we ought to be trying something new. In effect, we are done in by our blind spots.

In travel this might be exemplified by the Thinker who becomes more and more critical of himself and others when his own rational solutions fall apart. This might occur when train connections don't work out, a reservation falls through, or directions fail. Likewise, healers who are too nurturing and ready to sacrifice often turn into wounded healers. This is the doormat-of-a-person who takes the blame for every breakdown as a result of anxiety over possible abandonment. Knowing your own destructive excesses is invaluable during travel.

*Thanks to Myra Zylstra for this observation. I call it Zylstra's Law.

Table 4–1
Voices of Limitation That Erupt in Travel

Voice of Limitation	Examples	Situations in Which Voice Might Erupt
Limited Resourcefulness	—not smart enough —don't know language —never been there before —might find myself stranded —might feel trapped —not a quick learner —wouldn't want to do that without a partner or spouse	—unplanned opportunity for adventure —making connection with locals —challenge of driving on left side of the road while in England —invitation to meet others and share in their customs —departure from travel plan that requires you to make adjustments
Limited Self-Authority, Knowledge	—don't have a guide —no information on that —need more information —might be rejected	—getting oriented in a strange city —trying a new sport with foreigners
Financial Jeopardy	—would be endangering family if I took this dream job —have dependents to consider —might lose my job if I took more vacation time —can't afford to violate my budget —time to go home; I didn't budget for this problem	—job opportunity abroad —you lose money or are robbed

Voice		
Voice of Conformity and Image	—might look foolish behaving like that —didn't bring the right clothing —that would violate the protocol or plan	—new food at a foreign restaurant —invitation to join others in their home
Physical Limitation	—too old for that —not strong enough —my back is too weak —might get sick	—opportunity to go on a hike, try a new sport —possibility of traveling alone to an appealing destination
Unloveability and Lack of Wholeness	—not attractive enough —need a partner for that —wouldn't want to offend my partner who might abandon me	—someone shows a romantic interest in you but you balk —fed up with your travel partner but unwilling to leave or confront them
Voice of Victimization	—people are nasty to me —life is unfair —I am weak and powerless —if I stand up for myself I will be squashed or abandoned	—problems with vendors, hotel managers —you are abused or mugged or your travel companions become abusive

4e. Create a Mandala Showing the Buddha Nature You Will Practice on Your Trip

Now that you have seen the mugshots of the shadow and reviewed how you practice Buddha nature, create a mandala showing the mindsets you would like to emphasize on your trip.

You may include several of the Buddhas in your mandala (as I do). For example, Explorer mindset might be your goal if you seek to improve your orienteering, Communicator if you are looking to practice your French or do a better job of communicating with travelmates. Likewise, Healer nature might be an emphasis if you view your trip as a challenge to your self-doctoring and are hoping to make progress in healing a wound, either physical or emotional. Feel free to make notations in your mandala of your specific interests, but remember that in Step 5 you will define travel intentions and objectives.

You can complete Step 4e in a slightly different way by identifying shadow responses you would like to transcend or manage with more awareness. For example, you might want to moderate a tendency to lash out at others (stilling your Destroyer tendencies). Similarly, you may wish to do a better job of controlling evangelism or refrain from judging those who might not measure up to your own standards.

If you do work the problem in this way, try to turn the negative shadow response back into a positive. Identify the Buddha that is best able to handle negative chatter and related shadow response. Mystic might be the one to deal with impatience, as he is infinitely patient and forbearing. Enlightened Warrior might be able to contribute to this effort with a dose of resolve and strength. The trick here, as with all travel intentions, is to cast each mission as a challenge to Buddha nature. Each of the Buddhas loves to rise to the occasion and loves to perform.

When you are done with this exercise, record your mandala in the front of your journal.

Table 4-2
Buddha Tendencies Toward Excess

Buddha Nature	Common Excesses	Shadow Identity that Takes Over
Artist	Irresponsibility, infatuation with novelty, and disdain for practicality, efficiency	Dilettante
Harlequin	Acting as though nothing is ever serious; infatuation with disguise; posturing; playing to an audience	Panderer, Con Artist
Communicator	Manipulating others, preying on their gullibility	Spin Doctor
Explorer	Overemphasis on resourcefulness, excessive risk-taking, obsession with adventure	Daredevil
Mystic	Evangelism and judgment of others, Sanctimony	Evangelist, Judge
Healer	Too much nurturing and codependency, self-abnegation, excess sacrifice	Wounded Healer
Enlightened Warrior	Too much will, overemphasis on physical, aggression, competitiveness	Destroyer
Thinker	Hypercriticism, cynicism, thinking when action is more appropriate	Cynic, Procrastinator

5
Intentions and Objectives

Your intentions are your conscious travel desires and interests. For many of us they start out as a raw unconscious impulse, perhaps for adventure, greater vitality, or simply escape. We might not know exactly what we need, only that we aren't getting it and that we need to be packing our bags. Sometimes it only takes a TV ad or travel poster to activate our *wanderlust.* And then suddenly we are surrendering to thoughts of snorkeling the Great Barrier Reef, sailing Cape Horn, or losing ourselves in the Louvre.

> *We are shaped and fashioned by what we love.*
> *-GOETHE*
>
> *You create your reality with your intentions.*
> *-GARY ZUKAV*

Living in Seattle, I find that I am most susceptible in late March when slivers of sunlight part the dreary overcast sky and beckon the first daffodils. The writer and rebel Henry Miller always seems to agitate me further. He is the voice of freedom, the voice of artistic rebellion, the voice of the expatriate writer living by his wits in Paris. If I stumble onto one of his books—and I always seem to when I am first infected—I get crazy as a loon, as agitated as a sparrow overdue at Capistrano.

The first effect is on Buddha as Explorer, who dives into maps and atlases and the travel section of the *New York Times.* And then Warrior grows restive at work, resisting new responsibilities and hatching plans for escape. It doesn't seem to matter what I am doing or how badly I need to be working. Job and career are the least of my concerns.

The other Buddhas are easily provoked. Buddha as Artist heads for the bookstore and pages through paintings of Provence by Van Gogh. Harlequin begins plotting out dramas on the Istanbul Express.

On one occasion I was smitten just as I learned that I was in the finals for a job with the Washington State Department of Ecology. I hadn't worked for several months and really needed this job, and yet the Buddhas were clamoring for a trip to Paris. My would-be employer informed me that I had been selected from among a large pool of candidates. In the same breath he told me that I needed to start immediately or the job would go to someone else.

"Immediately?" replied a feeble, plaintive voice inside. I was sure that if I brought up Paris he would take back the offer. Just as I was about to surrender, Henry Miller erupted again with one of his shaming declarations about freedom:

"The language of society is conformity: the language of the creative individual is freedom."

"I won't be available for three weeks," I answered.

"We need you now," he replied more than a little irritated.

"Sorry, but that just isn't possible."

Immediately a meeker voice admonished, *"Are you nuts? Take the job and be glad anyone will hire you."*

"Look Mr. Currie, if you aren't here right away, we'll have to hire someone else."

"I guess we should talk about this tomorrow."

Later that day a friend of mine, who first introduced me to the works of Henry Miller and always supported my artistic rebellions, not-so-innocently presented me with a map showing all of Miller's favorite Paris haunts.

That evening I fell asleep imagining myself in Montparnasse sipping espresso while writing scenes from a novel in progress. I was surrounded by artists and emigré writers debating Sartre and Huxley. I was in heaven. Around midnight all the Buddhas rioted, falling into songs of rebellion from the hit musical *Marat/Sade.* Agent-provocateur Henry Miller was leading the refrain: *"We want our rights and we don't care how. We want our revolution. Now!"* In twilight I awakened to the sound of gunfire in the Marais where Frenchmen draped in the Tricolor were taking to the barricades.

My return call to Olympia was brief. "If you want me for the job, fine. We can talk about it when I get back from Paris. I'll be leaving tomorrow."

I waited for the hammer to fall. The manager seemed shocked by my reckless intemperance. Perhaps he was also considering how he might spread the word to the rest of the world that I was a shiftless slacker and a flake. Oh well, I would somehow survive. After all, Henry Miller had survived on fumes during the depression in Paris.

"Well, exactly when will you be back?" came the irritated reply.

"In four weeks, give or take."

Incredibly he wanted to know if the money and benefits were adequate. I had hardly opened my mouth when he sweetened the offer with more money, a four-day work-week, and a private office. "You will call us immediately when you return?" he asked solicitously when I refused to commit to an exact day.

"Oh, sure," I answered, more concerned about streaking to the airport.

On the plane I returned to that phone call: why had he rolled to his back like such a lap dog? I guess I had convinced him that I was someone worth waiting for. He was probably used to groveling applicants ready to accept whatever meager crumbs he dropped at their feet.

Much later I saw a *Seinfeld* episode in which George Costanza did something similar with George Steinbrenner, owner of the New York Yankees, who was interviewing applicants for a dream job. Steinbrenner had expected Costanza to grovel like the others, but Costanza did just the opposite—rebuking Steinbrenner for a series of brainless trades. From Steinbrenner came the reply: "Hire this man!"

I guess you never know what will happen when you take your direction from heartful intention and *are prepared to suffer the consequences.* This is the key. In my case I had resolved that the trip came first and I was willing to make all necessary sacrifices. No doubt this communicated strength, and certainly in the business world this is respected. On a spiritual level I also opened myself up to the abundance of the universe. I had practiced good Karma by aligning actions with inner spirit.

This latter point deserves emphasis. Intention that is harmonious with spirit, individual and collective, is the kind that taps into abundance and opportunity. When you are doing what you care about, you also tend to be motivated. Both of these reasons explain why opportunity seems to come to those who follow their bliss, as Joseph Campbell advised.

Planning and Preparation: Put the Buddhas to Work

Planning your trip is an opportunity to put your Buddhas to work for you. Most of them have special talents that can be used to shape intention, clarify strategy, orchestrate logistics, and get you through and around the barriers that block your way to the airport or open road.

Clarifying Travel Intentions

In the *Seat of the Soul,* the writer Gary Zukav speaks of intention as shaping the light that passes through us. At first, travel intentions are usually no more than basic impulses.

Some of the Most Basic Travel Interests

- romance
- escape
- relaxation or renewal
- broaden horizons
- adventure or discovery
- business
- family get-togethers
- pilgrimages

Looking back on my travels as a twenty- and thirty-year-old, I realize I was mostly motivated by the possibility of adventure. I loved the thrill of being in a strange place and making connections with people from other countries and fellow travelers. Then, too, I was drawn to the possibility of an exotic romance. I always seemed to meet bright, attractive women on my trips, which was seldom the case at home.

In recent years, my trips have emphasized creative expression and intellectual curiosity, particularly work on novels or art or my own interest in spiritual living. I am also interested in meeting people, but I have come to realize that travel romance also leads to travel complications and detours that you may regret later when the spell of infatuation breaks.

It's difficult if not impossible to incarnate Buddha as Artist, Explorer, Healer, or Mystic when your head is spinning with arousal.

Trips to the Louvre give way to trips to the bedroom. And even if you do get to the Louvre, you are apt to be more interested in your new friend's mesmerizing smile than that of the Mona Lisa. Almost always, signing up for romance distorts your experience and in some way diverts you from a once-in-a-lifetime opportunity. This isn't to suggest that your trip should be initiated with a vow of celibacy and non-involvement, only that you should be mindful of the risks and opportunity costs. (See chapter 9 for more on this.)

Step 5. Identification of Intentions and Objectives

Just as you can shape and focus your intentions to realize new opportunities, so can you amplify the power of an intention by deeper probing and clarification. For example, your basic interest might be a travel adventure in Europe, perhaps hiking in the Alps. You can deepen this by defining a specific objective and simultaneously considering how the objective answers an inner need.

Below in table 5-1 I illustrate how this might work.

Table 5–1
Intentions and Objectives of the Trip

Basic Interest	Objectives	Deeper Intention
1. Adventure in Europe—hiking or climbing	Mountain climbing with friends at Mt. Blanc or the Matterhorn	Affirmation of vitality, resourcefulness; lessened ego protection; mindfulness of Explorer; Communicator
2. Travel solo by train through Europe	Eurail trip to five countries in thirty days; go to Paris, Berlin, Amsterdam	Self-identification; resourcefulness; adaptability; self-acceptance; practice mindfulness of Explorer
3. Romance in Paris	Significant encounter or relationship	Greater vitality; love; greater wholeness
4. Explore/experience Venice.	Visit sites would have seen with Mom; practice artwork	Wholeness, grieving, experience silent witness; mindfulness of Mystic
5. Study art in great museums	Study works in the Louvre, Musée d'Orsay, Provence, and Van Gogh country	Wholeness, thirst for expression or knowledge, focus on Buddha as Artist and related mindfulness
6. Relaxation—recovery from job burn-out	Maui trip; relax on beach	Detoxify from job at odds with spirit; nurture self; work on Buddha as Healer
7. Immerse self in French culture	Live in Paris for two months, experience culture; read; work on language; classes at Sorbonne	Renew identity as Explorer, Communicator; spark intellectual curiosity; mindfulness of Communicator, Thinker, Explorer
8. Pilgrimage	Go to Lourdes; renew faith; study texts	Inspect self-authority work through beliefs and uncertainties; mindfulness of Mystic, Thinker
9. Environmental service; nature experience	Go to rainforest and work on revegetation or botanical medicine research project	Make a contribution to planetary health; connect with a larger community; affirm identity as Healer

In reviewing the table you'll note that column 2 (objectives) gives greater substance to a basic interest or impulse (column 1). Likewise, column 3 probes more deeply to define how the promotion of Buddha nature might or might not be embodied in the objective. Often we set our sights for a particular place or on a particular activity thinking that it will give us something that it can't. For example, beneath a desire for physical adventure (for example, scaling the Matterhorn) may lie a desire for more vitality or greater resourcefulness.

Take time to consider the spiritual aspects of your objectives. A felt-need for resourcefulness may actually reflect a feeling of vulnerability or powerlessness. If this is the root motivation for scaling the Matterhorn, the gain is likely to be short-lived. No amount of rock climbing is going to help you scale this mountain. Some deeper work may be in order to confront shadow voices of limitation. If you make this effort you may sensitize yourself to what you really need and the kinds of people and events that can really help you. Perhaps you may still head for the Alps but it will be with a different kind of sensory awareness. Should a slightly overweight fellow in a saffron robe amble through the lodge, you may notice. And if he drops a pearly insight that speaks directly to your need, you won't miss it as a result of being too focused on waterproofing your boots and testing your ropes.

Think Process Not Product

In creating and refining objectives also think in terms of process, not just product. How do you want to spend your day? What kind of interaction do you want with the people around you? How much time do you want on your own? What kind of thoughts do you want to be thinking in the morning, afternoon, and evening?

Much of your trip will be defined by the thoughts that are cycling through your brain day and night. Often people ignore this in trip planning. They imagine that simply by being elsewhere they will escape the problems that are troubling them at home—problems at work, problems with family or relationships, problems with money. And then when they arrive at their destination, the old wheels start spinning again.

As you may recall from Touchstone 9 (in chapter 3), we all have a tendency to replay our unresolved dramas. If our shadow is in control in Seattle, it is bound to run amok in Paris and Amsterdam when we are under travel stress.

To prepare for this, consider blowing up your objectives to reflect what you hope to be thinking about and how you will be spending your time. I have exemplified this in table 5–2.

This requires a bit of visualization. Consider a Eurail trip. What do you want to be giving your attention to? Try to be realistic, remembering that a good deal of your time will be spent getting to and from destinations, which can be taxing and agitating when you are disoriented and confused. If you are going to be staying in youth hostels, imagine how you might deal with noise and crowding. If you are traveling at the height of tourist season consider the strain of waiting in line and dealing with pushy people. The challenge here is to clarify and define the mindset you will practice in different situations.

It is also a good idea to think about your overall time allocation. I have given some particulars in column 3 to help you jog your thinking. The idea here isn't to create a detailed time budget but to consider some of the time demands that will be placed on you and how you will nurture your spirit.

Table 5–2
Relating Objectives to Mindset and Time Allocation

Objectives	Process Aspects and Mindset	Preferred Time Allocation
Eurail Trip to five countries in 30 days; go to Paris, Berlin, Amsterdam; practice mindfulness of Explorer.	State of mind : Minimum of encumbrances, freedom and spontaneous connections; stay in hostels, travel light; forbearing attitude toward self and others; don't sweat small stuff. Notes: 1. Enjoy meals; avoid scarfing them down. 2. When conversing with others try to be attentive and allow give and take (invoke Buddha as Communicator) 3. Don't allow self to be too agitated by rowdy young people on trains or at hostels. 4. Tune in to the dramas. They will be everywhere.	Train days: 4 hours of travel (max); max. of 1 hour spent getting to hotel and checking in; 2–3 hours of exploration; 2 hours writing; 1 hour eating and preparing meals. Non-train days: 3–4 hours exploration; 2–3 hours writing, reflecting; 2 hours eating, preparing meals.

Allowing the Trip to Shape Intention

Quite often deeper spiritual intention only crystallizes over the course of a trip. We might not know exactly what we need but the trip and mindful reflection illuminate it. I am reminded of a favorite folk tune by Reilly and Maloney: "I Got the I Don't Know What I Want, But I Ain't Getting It, Blues."

With a bit of self-awareness you can prompt your Buddhas to help you define what you need and want. I had such an experience on my trip to Europe in 1998.

This was a particularly tumultuous year for me. My mother died of cancer and chemotherapy after a harrowing drama in a Seattle hospital. In her final hours I made the difficult decision to disconnect her from life-support.

I was still working my way through my grief when I decided to break for Europe. My travel intentions were ill-defined. I suppose on a gut-level I was looking for escape from pressing obligations that I felt unable to handle. Maybe I was also looking for renewal. I certainly felt drained and discouraged and my faith in people was at an all time low.

A week before leaving I purchased a ticket to London with an open-ended return. Two days before I left I also purchased a Eurail Pass. My crude itinerary was to visit a friend outside of London, then head for the Continent and aimless train travel.

After two weeks in England, I flew to Copenhagen. I had been traveling uneventfully for seven days when I realized that I lacked the *joie de vivre* and enthusiasm of previous trips. Moreover, I hadn't really met anyone interesting and felt little desire to extend myself. It almost seemed pointless to continue. I was just wasting money.

Then a very queer thing happened. I fell ill with pneumonia. This was the illness that my mom finally died from. Near the town of

Aarhus I found myself a warm single room in a youth hostel and hunkered down, nursing myself with naturopathic medicine and trying to stay warm. (I wasn't about to check into a hospital.) For five days I was so sick I began to wonder whether I might die. In the process I relived much of the trauma suffered by my mom in her final days.

This might seem a little black and maudlin and the worst possible way to spend a vacation, but actually it was just the opposite. The discomfort and suffering brought me closer to my mom's spirit and allowed me to plumb my own grief and examine my core beliefs.

Just when I was sure that I was going down for the count (my breathing was down to about 25 percent of capacity), I experienced a remarkable turnaround. It came in the middle of the night after I encountered my mom in a dream. Both of us were pure spirit and connecting in a way described in the *Tibetan Book of the Dead*. It was like a homecoming in which all ego vanished. Nothing passed between us but pure love. I don't know if it was an out-of-body experience, but it was unusually powerful and lucid.

I awakened coughing but my fever had broken and I was breathing more deeply.

A day later, feeling almost normal, I caught a train from Hamburg to Bern and reflected on the experience and what I could draw from it. A fledgling belief in the immortality of the spirit (and many of my touchstones described in chapter 2) had been confirmed. I might not be ready to give up all my grief, but I was now convinced that my mom's spirit survived. This was no raw possibility, and not simply a matter of wishful thinking. I was as certain of it as my own existence. Moreover, the gap between life and death no longer seemed such a fearful and unfordable abyss. I was sure that in this lifetime there would be other moments when I would be able to touch my mom's spirit.

South of Freiburg, Germany, it dawned on me that I had just discovered the real intention of my trip. It wasn't about adventure in the usual sense, but about spiritual exploration by way of my own grieving process. Maybe I should embrace this intention—maybe even find a way to consecrate it.

How could I do this? Perhaps I could celebrate my mom's spirit by going somewhere that she would have loved—perhaps a place where we might have shared our common interest in art. We had talked about this a few months before she died.

The ideal destination was obvious—Venice. Mom loved water and would have delighted in painting the canals and studying the works of the Renaissance masters in the great Venice galleries.

From that moment on, the trip became joyful and exuberant and was electrified with synchronicity. In Venice the coziest, quaintest hotel I had ever seen was waiting for me. I chanced upon it while exploring scenes for a drawing. The manager informed me that he almost never had openings but a woman had just canceled out.

Bordering the hotel was a peaceful scenic canal that would have thrilled my mom. It was arched by several sculpted footbridges which sequestered several handcarved wooden boats, each with unique personality. The scene inspired a series of sketches that marked a leap in my drawing ability.

Across the Grande Canal at Saint Marco, I met several other artists on a trip to study and render the city. They were eager to pass on insights about perspective, color, and brushwork.

Upon leaving Venice I thought I was ready to return home and made my way to Milan to catch my scheduled return flight to the States.

At the airport I found myself in the midst of anarchy and mass hysteria. A general strike was taking place and it was every man, woman, and lama for himself. Giving in to survival instinct, I fought my way to the front of a line and flashed my ticket at the besieged and disheveled ticket seller. She shook her head with derisive amusement. "No way. There's only one flight a day to the States and you're only stand-by. Forget it."

I recovered with a plaintive, "What am I supposed to do?" while five other people clamored for her attention.

"Get to Paris—that's the only way you're getting home on this ticket."

How was I supposed to get to Paris—sprout wings? Then it dawned on me—my Eurail Pass wouldn't expire for two more weeks—the trains would get me to Paris. In fact, I might as well take a brief side-trip to Brittany. Yes, that would give me time on the train to clarify what had been going on behind the scrim in this eruptive unpredictable adventure.

It was a terrific side-trip that offered time for writing and reflection. In the process I realized the importance of probing the dramas that lie in the shadows. They tug on us, talk to us, and in some cases may even drown us if we don't pay attention. And yet if we do pay attention they can inform us about our undiscovered wholeness—parts of our higher self that we are struggling to realize on our travel path.

6
Strategy and Preparation

A s important as your intentions is your strategy for realizing them. It should give substance and practicality to your intentions and point you down a travel path that will nurture you emotionally and spiritually.

Release your specifications and say to the Universe:"find me where you know I need to be." Let them go and trust that the Universe will provide, and so it shall.

-GARY ZUKAV

Step 6. Setting a Travel Budget and Identifying a Strategy

Effective strategy always requires working with limitations. You will only have so much time and so much money and should budget it carefully. You also need to consider tradeoffs, as every choice you make will occasion some opportunity cost. For example, you might desire both comfort and mobility, but if you pack too much, the weight will hold you back: even a Buddha of Schwarzenegger proportions will have trouble ambulating through the streets of Paris, Barcelona, or London with a piano on his back.

In developing a strategy, focus on priorities and the big picture. I

"Maybe with the right mantra I can turn this into a feather."

do this by answering what I call "primary questions," which relate to money/resources, travel with partners, load considerations, security concerns, mode of transportation, and important contingencies.

Primary Questions for Strategy Development
　　How much money will I budget for the overall trip?
　　How much cash will I bring?
　　How much will I rely on credit cards, ATM withdrawals, or traveler's checks?
　　How will I mix modes of transportion on different legs of my trip—train, boat, plane, and so on?
　　Where will I stay and at what comfort level?
　　Will I be traveling alone or with friends/spouse?

Are my travel needs and interests compatible with those of my
    companions?

How light will I travel?

How will I fortify my health before and during travel?

What flexibility will I build into my travel plan?

What are my backup plans for replacing critical documents, such as
    passport or visa?

How will I protect myself from theft, muggings, sexual harassment, and
    unwanted attention?

Will I be speaking a foreign language and if so how will I prepare for it?

How will I fortify my spirit and support my unique emotional needs?

How will I respond to medical emergencies?

A number of other less critical questions (which I call secondary)
deserve consideration before your departure. They relate mostly to the
efficiency of travel and choosing among options once you are on the
road.

Secondary Strategy Questions

What can I jettison to increase my mobility?

Where and when will I be eating out or preparing my own food?

What are my opportunities to save money or to use it most efficiently?

How will I maintain enough privacy for reflection?

What deviations from my itinerary might enable me to capture more
    opportunity?

What feedback can I gain along the way to make improvements in my
    travel plan?

Don't feel compelled to write out answers, just look the questions over and imagine how they might apply to your trip. Simply by bringing them to conscious attention you anchor them in your subconscious, "putting a man on the job" (one or more of the Buddhas). Later, during your trip, if a question takes on importance, an answer will readily pop to the surface because the Buddhas have been dutifully considering options.

The details of standard travel planning are addressed in many travel guides, such as *Let's Go, Frommer's,* and *Europe Through the Back Door.* A number of books also discuss self-protection and the unique security needs of women traveling alone. The U.S. State Department also offers a number of publications that can help you prepare for travel contingencies. In the pages that follow I provide a variety of other tips based on past experience and the suggestions of seasoned travelers.

After you answer the primary questions, record your strategy and budget in the front of your journal. (You will need 1 to 2 pages.)

Budgeting

An important element of strategy is budgeting. A budget can either be an aid to mindfulness or a terrible albatross that restricts your freedom. I try to follow a few basic principles in my budgeting as listed below.

Budgeting Principles
1. *Create a budget that gives you the ability to monitor significant variable expenditures.*
2. *Set your levels at amounts compatible with the mindset that your are trying to achieve.*
3. *Recognize the variability of local costs. Big cities will cost more.*

4. View your budget as a guideline, not a strait jacket.

5. Create surplus during flat periods when nothing is really happening and there is no imperative to spend.

6. Allow yourself to spend surplus on special opportunities.

Most people like to set a ceiling for routine daily expenditures (for example, $75 a day). This may or may not include big-ticket items (such as airfare, train passes). My own convention is to exclude such elements from the daily target because they distort it. The value of the budget is that it gives you power over variable expenditures, but train passes and airline tickets are generally fixed.

It is useful to establish targets for lodging, food, and entertainment because these account for significant variable costs. I don't strictly enforce category expenses, but by tracking them I am able to determine the main reasons why my trip is costing more or less than expected.

In general, I only view my budget and daily targets as fixed and inviolable when my resources are extremely limited. (A few years back this was the way I traveled. Now I have more cushion.) Over time I have also discovered the value of adjusting my spending to my developing opportunities. On almost all lengthy trips, flat periods will occur (or transitions between adventures) when nothing seems to be happening and there is no point in spending to targets. In such cases I accumulate a reserve to spend on something special, for example, dinner with a new acquaintance or a side-trip.

Traveling Alone vs. Traveling with Others

Traveling with a significant other will change your experience. Different people will be attracted to you, and you in turn are likely to engage others in a different way. For me there is a time and place for traveling solo versus ensemble, and this is best determined by close consideration of intentions, not only mine but those of potential travelmates.

It is always tempting and often misleading to assume that you and your mate are looking for the same things and want to travel in the same way. Two friends of mine, Robert and Rachel, traveled together for forty years and only recently realized that they needed to give each other more space. Although both are artists and enjoy painting and photography, they pursue them differently. Robert is a perfectionist about natural light and is willing to wait endlessly for changes in cloud cover and sun angle. Rachel is less demanding.

Rachel and Robert also have different views about driving. Robert is the ultimate road warrior and from dawn to sunset likes to cover as much mileage as possible. She prefers a more leisurely pace with sight-seeing along the way, which always causes Robert to chafe.

For several years Rachel made all the concessions, traveling Robert's way without complaint. Finally her resentment surfaced and a fight erupted. Eventually they were able to talk out the problem and find common ground. Now they give each other more time on their own for artwork, and car travel never begins without ground rules and an overall plan. On occasion they also take separate vacations.

Problems such as these are common when people travel together, even people who know each other well. Partly this is because travel stresses bring out differences and incompatibilities, also because couples are often not aware of their own tacit conventions for solving problems. One of the most common conventions is for one person to give another options and for the other to make the choice. Alternatively, each person might take the lead in a certain area (for example, map-reading, cooking, finding suitable accommodations, and so on).

Problems arise when the convention changes without mutual agreement, the convention does not cover a particular problem, or one person mutinies.

Below are some of the decision-making questions you should consider with your companion before departure and carry forward into your strategy.

Important Issues to Consider when Traveling with Spouse or Friend
> What is absolutely essential to each of us? (for example, seven hours' sleep, a hot shower in the morning)
>
> What are the special skills and strengths of each of us? (for example, exchanging money, reading maps, driving, foreign language, cooking, and so on)
>
> How are these skills going to be reflected in our decision-making?
>
> What decisions will be delegated and which ones shared?
>
> How closely are we going to stick to our itineraries?
>
> What kind of criticism is out of line?
>
> How early do we get started in the morning?
>
> How are we going to talk to one another when a conflict arises?

A critical issue is how you and your mate will deal with stress and conflict. For example, if I don't like your idea for navigating through the streets of Paris or using the Metro map, how can I let you know? Do I have to soft-pedal my opposition? You should note also that what one considers smooth, another considers stressful. For example, I fully expect some amount of disorientation when I arrive in a European city for the first time. I expect to get lost on the way to my hotel from the central train station and rely upon locals to set me straight. More than a few travelmates who figured I was some kind of expert have found this unnerving to the point that it has even scuttled our partnership. I now try to do a better job of anticipating and preventing this kind of misunderstanding by explaining my impairment in advance.

Codependency is a particularly nettlesome issue for many travelers. Mates often fall into relationships in which one person takes on the role of enabler, supporting the other person's addiction. The specific addiction doesn't really matter. On the surface it could be about alcohol, gambling, taking wild risks, sex, or the like. On a more fundamental level it is always about shrunken divinity, fear of life and death, and out-of-control ego. The enabler's payoff is that he or she isn't abandoned. (The enabler's greatest fear is to be alone and powerless.)

Traveling with a codependent is especially difficult because uncertainties are bound to arise that create stress and bring out the worst in each partner. Think twice about traveling with a codependent unless you have both decided that you are going to use travel as a vehicle to repair your relationship. Never, ever, consider traveling with someone who is unable to talk candidly about a developing conflict or who is callous to your needs.

Packing for Light Travel

What you bring along, including luggage and clothing, should reflect your travel objectives, but it always helps to think in terms of efficiency and utility. This is especially important on Eurail trips when you don't have the luxury of dropping luggage in the trunk of a car or giving it to a taxi driver.

When backpacking I place the highest priority on items that will be used repeatedly, are light, and protect me from the elements. I take much of my direction from Australians and New Zealanders who are among the best backpackers in the world. (This seems to derive from the fact that they commonly go on lengthy trips and put more thought into efficient travel.) If you meet one of them along the road, ask what they are carrying and if they have any special tips.

Backpacks

If you are backpacking, invest in a waterproof pack that is easy on your back, contains a waist strap, and allows attachment of a sleeping bag or sleeping sack. An inefficient pack that rides too low or is too bulky can make life miserable. Toting "the Steinway" is a frequent mistake of young male travelers who think that simply because they can lift the piano they can carry it to Timbuktu without any ill effects. Over the course of a long trip, the piano always defeats the body. If your back and neck survive you may end up with blistered feet, aching knees, or a cold caused by your failure to change clothes after you were drenched in sweat. Backpacking should not be arduous exercise unless you view this as part of your adventure and plan accordingly.

Another problem with "piano"-packs is that they often demand piano storage. Most of them won't fit in the overhead compartment of a plane or under a seat. Also, lockers at train stations are often not large enough to accommodate them.

Pay particular attention to shoulder straps and zippers. Straps should be padded and zippers should be strong enough to withstand stress. Only invest in metal ones and test them out on a full pack. Note also that waist straps can redistribute some of the load from back, neck, and shoulders to hips and midsection.

Rick Steves sells an excellent multipurpose, frameless pack for around $120. It can also be converted to carry-style luggage, which gives you the option of looking more presentable to people who might judge you by appearance (namely, hotelkeepers).

Note also that when backpacking it is a good idea to bring along a small day-pack. It should be large enough to carry literature, lunch, your journal, and a few clothing items (for example, your rain jacket). I recommend a nylon pack as it will take up less space in your main pack.

Clothing Considerations

Nylon underwear is preferable to cotton because it dries quickly, which is important if you have limited access to laundry facilities. Both nylon and wool socks have advantages and disadvantages so I carry both. Wool, of course, provides insulation even when wet, but is bulkier and not apt to dry overnight when you don't have access to an electric dryer.

Good rain gear is indispensable and should be a high priority if you travel in climates with a moderate-to-high probability of rain. Even if you have to pay more, always invest in high quality material that breathes, such as Gortex. Here are some of my priority considerations in selecting a raincoat:

Raincoat Criteria
> 1. *Gortex or a kindred material is preferable to coated nylon.*
> 2. *Make sure that the seams are waterproof.*
> 3. *Make sure that the zippers are sturdy. Avoid plastic rails.*
> 4. *Make sure that the coat reaches to mid-thigh. Otherwise bring along rain pants. (I do anyway.)*

5. *Make sure the coat is lined (this prevents the accumulated moisture from chilling you).*
6. *Look for inner pockets that can be used to store valuables.*
7. *Make sure that the hood is adjustable and has a small bill.*
8. *Look for vents that can be opened to cool you down when you exert.*
9. *Look for a waist drawstring that you can tighten to reduce heat-loss in cold weather.*
10. *Make sure that the coat is large enough so that you can layer.*

Layering is vastly superior to traveling with a single-purpose, heavy-duty parka. Remember that you will be sweating more when you carry a pack. Moisture and temperature control are usually the biggest problems of new backbackers. Layering allows you to shed as you grow warmer and to find an equilibrium at which you are neither cold nor hot.

Consider the need for shedding when you choose sweaters, shirts, and other items you will use as layers. Once you are on the road you are apt to decide that some piece of clothing is not worth its weight. You will be reluctant to shed it if it is too expensive. For this reason my layers often include my ugliest sweaters.

Shoe Considerations

Shoes deserve special emphasis for any trip on which you are bearing a load. Remember that footfall is where most friction occurs. Toes, feet, ankles, and knees will suffer from poor shoes or boots. Never use a trip to break in a new pair of shoes. Also think "functionality" rather than "lookin' good."

My travel shoes must meet strict design parameters:

Desirable Features in Travel Shoes
  1. *composite sole with give and nonslip gridding*
  2. *low-cut design for lightness (my ankles are strong)*
  3. *external laces (just in case I need to replace them)*
  4. *waterproof seams with thread stitching between the sole and the upper*
  5. *soft but heavy-duty leather uppers, inside cushioning to absorb impact.*

I satisfy these criteria with a top-of-the-line pair of Timberland or Eccos. With a little polish I can make myself presentable for an evening in a Monte Carlo club or at a Paris soirée.

A second pair of shoes is necessary if you spend considerable time outdoors in rain, snow, or around water. I find that a broken-in pair of basketball shoes meets my needs and those of most other male back-packers. The leather outers provide rain protection, and the shoes are usually supple enough to be stuffed in my pack. A bonus is that Buddha is thereby equipped for a high-flying game of basketball should Michael Jordan appear and lay down a challenge for a game of one-on-one (a mistake because the Buddha soars). The needs of women travelers may vary from those of men, particularly if they plan to wear a dress. In this case consider if your primary shoes will suffice, otherwise an additional (third pair) may be necessary.

Tools and Accessories

A Swiss Army knife is a must. It should contain a Phillips and regular-head, can opener, file, and large knife. The scissors attachment is Mickey Mouse, so don't pay for it. Also don't worry about the metal utensils. You can get by just fine with plastic or steel utensils available at hostels.

Other important items to consider include the following: a small durable flashlight, string, bungee straps, a small roll of strong tape, pen and pencil, thread and needle, a number of Ziploc bags of different sizes, a watch with alarm, and a garbage bag. The string can double for shoe laces and provide a clothes line. The knife can be used for protection and food preparation. The Ziploc bags can protect important materials from the rain or keep food from wetting your clothing. The garbage bag serves the same purpose and can be used as a laundry bag and ground cloth.

Sometimes it is useful to carry a combination lock, but you should consider whether the weight is justified. Most train-station lockers already have good locks. In some hostels you may have to provide your own, but often you can purchase one there.

"Buddha levitates over Michael Jordan."

Miscellaneous Items

Forget about detergent, spices for food, canned goods, and perishable food that you won't be eating immediately. You can pick up these items when you need them. I used to carry a sleeping bag but discovered I couldn't justify it. I rarely sleep outside and a bag is unnecessary at a hostel. The more important need is a sleeping sack which will save you charges at a hostel and give you hygienic bedding when you stay in cheap hotels.

Good maps and a travel guide are a must on any European backpacking trip. I always include a large map of Europe as well as smaller blow-ups of a few destinations. I also supplement with local maps when I arrive at my destination.

For a more complete discussion of packing considerations refer to *Let's Go, Europe Through the Back Door,* and other travel guides.

Staying Healthy and Planning for Emergencies

Health concerns should be paramount in your planning. Consider the fact that trips exact stress by way of fatigue and exposure to germs and toxins.

Health Stresses during Travel

1. *If you travel by plane you will be breathing recycled air.*
2. *Water may lack adequate purification or vary greatly in natural purity, including mineral content.*
3. *You probably won't sleep as restfully as when you are on your own mattress.*
4. *Your system may not be acclimated to local temperature and humidity.*

5. *You may be in a location where different pathogens are present in air, water, and food, and your immune system is not yet resistant to them.*

6. *Locally grown food may contain toxins (for example, pesticides) which further stress your system.*

7. *Food preparation may not adhere to the same health standards.*

8. *You are apt to exert more energy during travel than when you are at home.*

9. *You may be more exposed to the elements and be chilled by perspiration.*

10. *Your system can be undermined by diet, which you have less control over than when you are at home.*

11. *Cigarette smoking is ubiquitous in public places outside the United States.*

You should know your own health sensitivities and prepare accordingly. Some preventive measures to consider in travel planning are the following:

Preventing Illness and Fortifying Health

1. *Before leaving consult with your doctor about any chronic or acute medical condition.*

2. *Build up your immune system.*

3. *Make sure you are getting optimal nutrition.*

4. *For special conditions that are not easily recognized by a doctor, wear a Medic Alert tag.*

5. *If sex is even a remote possibility, pack condoms.*

6. *Bring along important prescriptions (which you may need to fill if your medicine runs out or is lost).*

7. *Prepare yourself for the possibility of diarrhea, especially when water quality is suspect, by bringing along appropriate over-the-counter medicine.*

8. *Inquire about local medical hazards by contacting The International Association for Medical Assistance to Travelers (417 Center St., Lewiston, NY 14092; U.S. phone: 716-754-4883). The association provides brochures and a directory of English-speaking doctors. A similar service is provided by the International Society of Travel Medicine (ISTM).*

9. *Check the coverage of your medical insurance. Policies often cover emergency care abroad but you can purchase supplemental coverage from different providers. One source of information is Travel Assistance International (202-821-2828). Note also that many host countries in Europe offer free medical care, but you may not get exactly what you want and may have to wait longer than you are accustomed.*

My own medical provisions always include a bottle of echinacea, vitamins, bee pollen, special herbs for allergies and breathing, aspirin, acidophilus, lip balm, eye drops, and a few Band-Aids. In summer I pack sunscreen. Note also that herbal concoctions are available to lessen the effects of jet lag and a variety of other travel ailments.

Everyone who travels for extended periods of time should develop a personal system for health and wellness monitoring that reflects individual needs and sensitivities. Although few of us are doctors, we can take the time to learn the basic pathways by which our individual maladies develop, be they influenza, allergies, asthma, digestive problems, skin disorders, or common infections. Ralph Golan, M.D., N.D., has written a handy and accessible reference book *(Optimal Wellness,*

Ballantine,1995) that I like to review before an extended trip. The book provides tips for diagnosis, fortifying health, and responding to illness.

Clean water is not a major concern in northern European countries but you should also be aware that simply because water is free from pathogens it is not necessarily pure. It may contain organic chemicals, metals, and asbestos. It may also be devoid of healthful minerals such as calcium and magnesium.

Trips in less developed countries require considerably more attention to water. Unless you are confident that the water is free from fecal pathogens and other microbes you should avoid eating uncooked or reheated food, raw salads, fruit you cannot peel, street-vendor food, fresh milk, and ice. Generally water from local sources should be boiled, and it may be necessary to treat it with purifiers. Even when I am in northern European countries, my preference is to drink bottled water, and I try to consume at least three quarts a day. If you plan to travel in the tropics, research potential problems with tropical diseases. One of the best sources is ISTM:

International Society of Travel Medicine
P.O. Box 871089
Stone Mountain, GA 30087-0028
Phone: 770-736-7060
Web site: http://www.istm.org

ISTM provides hotlinks to groups with specialized expertise in tropical medicine such as the World Health Organization, Centers for Disease Control, and the Traveler's Medical and Vaccination Center Group (Australia).

A must for any backpacker is diligent foot care. Inspect your feet regularly and protect against blisters, ingrown nails, and so forth. I always carry a small tube of Vaseline petroleum jelly to keep my feet lubricated. If you are backpacking, assume that your feet are going to blister unless you keep them lubricated. Nothing can be so vexing as to arrive at an enchanted place that begs for exploration, only to discover that your feet are a bloody mess and that you need to stay off them.

To prevent a cold, the flu, or a more serious infection, monitor your fatigue and energy level. Before you leave consider your unique sensitivities (that you should capture in your health barometer).

On my own trip in 1998, I underestimated my general fatigue and stress, which were high even before my arrival in Europe. A few weeks into my trip I overtaxed myself with a night in a smoky bar with a group of wild Scandinavians. The next day I came down with pneumonia.

I'm sure I could have prevented this if I had thought about my condition more carefully. I knew, for example, that I was particularly susceptible to cigarette smoke and that my breathing was already labored. I also experienced difficulty getting over jet lag. It was perfectly predictable that a late night out would do me in.

Fortifying Your Spirit (with Books, Music, and So On)

Since most of my trips emphasize art and writing, I also pack drawing pencils and carry at least one good book to stir my imagination. I reconcile myself to the fact that along the way I will finish the book and pass it on. Predictably another book will arrive from the cosmos just after I have orphaned my own. I'll find it on a train, in a locker, or in a restaurant.

Another important need is music, for me a recent discovery. I now travel with a Walkman cassette player and a few favorite cassettes. This soothes the various Buddhas when they are under assault from voices of limitation or marooned in Italian stations during strikes. A bonus is that the music can muffle snoring in a hostel sleeping-room. I would pack a musical instrument if I could, but this would cause alarms to go off: Buddha as Explorer holds me to a strict weight limit of 15 kilograms.

Protecting Yourself and Your Valuables with a System

A wealth of information is available in books and on the Internet about self-protection during travel. One of the best web sites is **www. travel-library.com,** which will link you to international consultants on travel security. Some of the tips apply to specific regions of the world while others are more general. Where you go, your gender, the style of your travel (for example, backpacking), the time of day you are traveling, and whom you are traveling with will all affect your risk and what you should take into account in creating a personal security system.

Differentiate between critical and noncritical valuables and place the highest priority on the protection of the former. These should include your passport, a credit card, cash, important prescriptions, travel tickets, and passes (such as a Eurail Pass). Store them in a large money belt or fanny pack. Wallets and purses are simply too easy to rip off.

Consider your own potential for absent-mindedness and accidents as much as the potential for theft. If you are like me you realize that senility can strike at any moment, causing you to misplace or damage important possessions.

You can protect against water damage by placing important papers in Ziploc bags. I always place my passport and air-ticket in a Ziploc bag inside my money belt.

Redundancy is critical for important documents and resources. Store a few days' worth of cash, an extra ATM card, and an extra photo I.D. in the bottom of your large pack or somewhere other than your money belt.

Routine is perhaps the most important aspect of a personal security system. For example, let's say that you store your critical valuables in your money belt or fanny pack. Your routine might be to check the contents every time you remove your passport, before you leave your hotel, or before you get on a train, plane, or boat. Your checking procedure should be akin to a pilot in preflight: "Wallet? Check." "Passport? Check."

A word about critical valuables: don't assume that a locked hotel door insures protection. You simply can't afford to take the chance that someone will break in, even if you are only down the hallway at the restroom. In fact the only time I remove my money belt is when I am showering or sleeping, and even then it is within arm's length.

Money belts are problematic if overloaded, in which case zippers may break or a belt that is not fully zipped may spill its contents. Part of the problem is that many belts are poorly balanced and easily invert. If you are going to purchase one, test it first, by filling it up completely and checking to see how it rides, and also how easily you can zip and unzip it. This will pay dividends later when you are making a run for a departing train and can ill afford to drop your valuables.

In developing my security system, I expect that at some point during my trip I will be in a crowd and someone will try to rip me off. One of the most common M.O.'s is a two-person ploy whereby someone distracts you (perhaps by bumping into you) while another cuts away your waist pack.

Buddha the Explorer is prepared for this. He connects a safety strap from my regular belt to my waist pack. If someone cuts away my waist-band I don't lose my money belt. In most locations you should also conceal your money belt by covering it with a shirt or coat.

Where you go, at what hour, and with how much weight can have a direct bearing on your security. Big cities at night can be especially hazardous for the solo traveler, particularly if you are in a high crime neighborhood. The weight you are carrying is important because it constrains your ability to escape. It also taxes your energy which can make you less alert and ready to deal with crisis.

As important as mobility is vision. Be mindful of what you can and cannot see. Be aware that your field of vision is reduced by a hooded raincoat.

Take advantage of train station lockers to lessen your load, especially when you are looking for lodging. You can always return later and pick up your pack after you have found a room. Of all the city stations, only those in Paris do not provide lockers (because of anti-terrorism regulations). Adjacent to Paris stations are hotels where you can usually stow your pack for a nominal charge.

I am especially watchful when I arrive late at night at the following stations: Dublin (main), Amsterdam (main), Paris Gare du Nord, Paris Gare de L'Est, London King's Cross, Hamburg, and Naples.

When you store your pack in lockers, avoid conversation or connections with strangers. Scam artists may help you with a key-lock and then switch keys with you. If you are traveling by car never leave valuables inside the car or trunk. These are easy targets for rip-off artists.

Remember that anonymity and invisibility are among the Buddha's best friends. (This is his Taoist side.) Never advertise yourself with bright and expensive clothing; wear minimal jewelry; and whenever possible blend into the crowd. Likewise, avoid removing money from your money belt when you are out in public or in a crowd.

Only if you really want to challenge your warrior skills will you advertise the fact that you are an American. If this is your interest consider wearing a bright Chicago Bulls T-shirt, Air Jordan Nike shoes, and a Planet Hollywood hat. You'll increase your popularity if you talk in loud Americanized English and fumble through a large wad of bills while drawing down a beer. The best places for such a performance are crowded piazzas and train stations, parades, discos, and popular tourist traps.

The perils of travel obviously vary by country, region, and the political crisis of the moment. If you are at all unsure about the safety

"Air Jordans have their disadvantages."

of travel in a foreign country, contact the U.S. State Department at your local federal building. The American Citizens Services also provides useful information.

American Citizens Services
2201 C. Street Northwest, Rm. 4811
Washington, D.C. 20520
Phone: 202-647-5225

When you are on the road, especially if you are on a long trip, monitor bulletins and notices by connecting to the Web or checking with the U.S. Consulate.

Loss of Important Documents

More than a few trips have been scuttled by the loss of a passport or visa. Besides protecting them as I have described above, invest in a bit of contingency planning. Bring along a spare photo I.D. and let a friend back home (who has access to your house or apartment) know the location of your birth certificate. The birth certificate may be required to replace your passport. In most cases your first step after losing a passport should be to report the loss to local police. They will usually provide you with temporary I.D. The U.S. Consulate or Embassy should also be contacted to help you replace documents. *Passport Office Publication M-264* describes visa requirements in foreign countries. Other publications list specific steps to follow in case of passport or visa loss.

Special Concerns of Solo Women Travelers

Women traveling alone face greater hazards than men and should therefore be more mindful of their surroundings and what can go wrong.

Avoid late night travel in subways and on other public transportation. Think about escape and flight whenever you are on the street, and evaluate the peril of your surroundings. In a big city your backpack should be stowed in a locker by dark.

In general, realize that what you take for granted in the States may not apply abroad, including the safety of door locks, the privacy of rooms, and the effectiveness of forcefully saying no.

Sometimes we are too politically correct to admit it, but harassment is more likely in some countries than others, such as Italy, Spain, and the Balkans. If these countries are on your itinerary, exercise extra caution.

Women should rule out hitchhiking in all countries and will always be safer traveling with known companions, male or female. Follow the Tao invisibility suggestions described above for reducing risks. Also avoid form-fitting pants and other clothing that may advertise your sexuality. Unfortunately in many cultures, a woman traveling alone is often perceived as being interested in a sexual encounter.

To prepare for contingencies, carry a whistle, and even before you arrive at a hazardous location, play out possible responses to difficult situations. Imagine, for example, how you might respond if someone in a crowd pinches or grabs you. In general, you should avoid eye contact with leerers and know the local vernacular for saying no in such a way as to leave no doubt about underlying intention. Always carry a flashlight at night and be ready with an ample phone card that you know how to use. The phone card will do you no good if you haven't figured out how to dial an operator or call the police. This can vary from place to place even within a single country.

Remember also that an awareness of local surroundings is critical. Stay away from dark streets and high-crime neighborhoods. Steer clear of walls during the night and watch your back. Avoid turning your back to the sidewalk when looking at buildings. If you sense you are entering a perilous block or neighborhood, don't hesitate to turn back and find a better route. Don't be afraid to hail a cop if you aren't sure of directions or are apprehensive about your surroundings.

In preparation for a solo trip, you should review the specialized literature and videos on female travel. These discuss specific harassment scenarios and the pros and cons of different emergency responses.

Strategies for Meeting the Right People

Connections with the right people figure prominently in most everyone's travel objectives. If you are interested in making new friends or acquaintances, consider where you will be staying and how you are traveling, as this will influence the kind of people who enter your sphere. Attitude is also critical. Mindful and aware people are more apt to gravitate to you if you project the same qualities.

Because I like to engage people in deep conversations, especially on art, writing, and spirituality, I typically arrange my vacation around an initial event such as a conference. This will attract people with like interests and quite often this will lead to some follow-up opportunity in which the connection will be deepened.

Once on the road and traveling solo, I try to be open and to practice the credo and skills of Buddha as Communicator. I find that Europeans are generally more public and outgoing than Americans (although this seems to depend on what parts of America and what parts of Europe you are visiting). Certainly large European cities have a long tradition of open conversation in cafes, pubs, *gasthauses,* and hostels. This also carries over to public transportation, particularly train travel.

Before trying to make contact with another traveler or local, I try to gauge that person's state of mind and general openness. It is against my travel credo to be invasive, and I try to be very sensitive about the desires of others to sleep, read, or engage in self-reflection. Observing someone's eyes is a good sign of his or her availability for conversation. Body language is also instructive.

Pursuing your own interests is also a good prescription for meeting kindred souls. I don't know how many people I have connected with simply because they noticed me reading what they thought was an interesting book or because they shared my interest in sketching.

7
Your Daily Log

Step 7. Maintain Your Log and Use It for Self-Reflection

Your log is not only a record of what has happened to you, it is your tool for active reflection, enabling you to become silent witness to the people, forces, and events swirling around you. The silent witness is the observer side of Buddha nature—the Mystic that finds spirit and meaning in what you experience, the Harlequin attuned to dramas around you, and the other Buddhas whom you may call on to make sense of the seen as well as the ineffable.

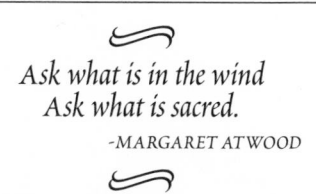

Ask what is in the wind
Ask what is sacred.
-MARGARET ATWOOD

It is easy to get carried away with journal keeping and forget its purpose. Remember, the intent is to deepen your travel drama and adventure, not to substitute for it. The last thing most people want on a vacation is to feel imprisoned by a self-inspection process.

At the same time, realize that memory and impression are perishable, especially for those of us without photographic recall, those of us who struggle to remember which day of the week it is. In this case your journal enables you to register important events so that at the appropriate moment you can reflect on them. In effect, your journal is like a thread that you spool out as you travel. At stops along the way you mark and color it with sensation and thought, and then when you are ready, you reel it back in to make sense of what has been happening to you.

Here are some of my own guidelines for journal keeping.

1. Don't let your journal control you.

Although it is often convenient to set aside time in late evening for an entry, you may then be too tired for anything more than listing events and basic financial accounting. Good writing and reflection take alertness that can be hard to muster late at night. I know that if I am fatigued from backpacking, my brain is disabled by 9 P.M. Insights at that hour can be measured in candlepower and if I want to capture the feeling and emotion of a visceral experience, my writing will be flat and listless.

You should never feel that your journal is a burden or that you are contractually bound to give it time. If opportunities arise to go out with friends, see a film, or join in a group discussion, catch up on your journal the next day. I know that if I had been strict about sticking to a late-night regimen, I would have missed out on some wonderful experiences.

2. Shoot for a minimal entry in which you record enough information for later reflection and probing.

A minimal entry before bed will take less than 15 minutes if you are well organized and develop a good system for recording daily events. My own is a kind of annotated chronology (which I describe in greater detail below). Before I give in to sleep I also like to rate my physical, emotional, and spiritual condition (applying my barometers), and quickly note the contributions of the different Buddhas to my adventures, people connections, and creative expression.

My chronology includes annotations that capture the emotion and feeling of each important event. I use various descriptors to tag or mark the event with emotion and sensation. This is very important. Once you mark an event, your subconscious begins to work on it. Though you may be sleeping or occupied by play or travel concerns, you are quietly integrating the experience with deeper intentions and with your store of knowledge and sensation.

This is the very process that explains most of the great break-throughs in science, the arts, and literature. It is sometimes referred to as seeding. You seed your unconscious with a marked thought and while you are engaged in other activities the seeds germinate.

The shoots that come to life are unpredictable. They may include deeper insights about your experience or creative brainstorms. My own have included ideas for novels, inventions, and works of art. Of course, different kinds of seeding are more or less effective and some seeding only turns out weeds and crabgrass, but that is all part of the process.

3. Don't force your entry to be a masterpiece.

It is easy to make the mistake of aspiring to such a high standard that journal keeping becomes a joyless chore: for example, deciding that your entries have to be brilliantly insightful and original. This is a pre-scription for abandonment. Remember that you aren't in competition with Thomas Wolfe or May Sarton. Your journal is only a tool to pro-mote your own mindfulness—to create a continuous record of thought, experience, and mindset that will add to your journey. My own entries are rarely more than fragments, and quite often full of grammatical abominations.

The same point applies to artwork—never feel that you have to create masterpieces. Even modest amateurish work has the effect of coloring and marking an experience and drawing out the emotions that you feel at a point in time. This deepens a travel experience and makes it unique. Later, if you want to turn a sketch into a masterpiece, go ahead.

Over time you will find that your expression will come more quickly and easily. You'll get the hang of drawing cathedrals, sketching cityscapes, and capturing an interesting personality. All the Buddhas must walk before they run and even before they can levitate they must learn to jump (à la mere mortals like Michael Jordan).

4. Bring imagination and exploration to your process.

The back of my journal is always full of letters to myself and friends, poems and doggerel, sketches and crazed inventions. Nothing is out of bounds. I take guidance from Leonardo's notebooks, Anais Nin's journals, and Henry Miller's artistic brainstorms.

Remember that playful exploration is the midwife of creative breakthrough. The key to any kind of brainstorming is willingness to let go of convention and rigid assumptions. Give yourself license to make strange connections; allow yourself to doodle and to associate spontaneously.

The human brain, consciously or unconsciously, is a master spider, habituated to spinning out links, comparisons, analogies, and integrations. Just give it license and it will begin shooting threads between the experiences you are having and your touchstones, between past events and present, between an image on a billboard and a drama you glimpsed on a subway platform or *marketplatz.*

5. Invite the Buddhas to sound off.

When you are empty of insight, which happens to all of us, go back and review the mindset of each Buddha. Look at both the credo and curiosities, then invite each of your spiritual companions to sound off. Buddha as Artist will soon be reaching for a pencil to create a portrait of someone you met at noon; Harlequin will begin defining your hidden dramas; Healer will begin a work-up on the current imbalance; and Mystic will go to work harmonizing intention and experience.

6. Find a special inner space for deeper probing.

The Buddha is said to have realized enlightenment beneath the Bodhi Tree in India; Thoreau had his Walden Pond; and Henry Miller and Carl Sandburg took inspiration from the seamy cityscapes of Paris and Chicago. Everyone has a special preference for the reflective pool that will evoke the silent witness. Find yours and go there when you are ready to probe more deeply, when you are confused or disoriented.

Many people convince themselves that these places must be substantial and physical—that they must visit Notre Dame and take communion with a priest wearing a funny hat. Or perhaps they need to be up to their knees in the Ganges in Benares. The truth is that all sacred places are really in the mind's eye and the pilgrim's heart. The Buddhas within don't really care where they are. They have no preference between the real and the imagined. Give them the illusion of wine as the blood of Christ and the Holy Ghost will fill them; give them the suggestion of flowing water and the Ganges will float their boat.

For Teresa of Avila such a place was called The Fourth Mansion. This was an inner house rather than a quaint cabin in the woods, and it was sanctified by the votive candles of her faith. Here she surrounded herself with beloved creatures, stilled the noise of ego, and took her communion. We can all transport ourselves to these mansions of the heart if we so desire.

One of the most compelling stories about sacred refuge is told by Viktor Frankl, the noted humanistic psychologist. He speaks of Jewish inmates at Auschwitz creating their own sacred inner space which Nazi evil couldn't penetrate. Here even the most downtrodden and abused bodies could come to renew faith and conviction.

With a little practice you can create your own retreat and it won't require a down payment for a plot of ground in the Adirondacks. The challenge is to disassociate physical setting with state of mind. See chapter 8 for an elaboration of techniques for meditation, visualization, and centering.

Minimal Entries
Basic Chronology and Annotations

The basic chronology is a record of daily events and experiences. Sometimes it is unadorned and only contains limited description, especially if nothing very significant happened. On other occasions more notes are provided that capture the feelings and sensations of experiences.

I try to move from outer to inner—from the physical experience and its raw characteristics to inner dramas and my own intentions. Here is an example from a particularly memorable day in Bavaria.

Sample Minimal Log Entry

9/20/94 Salzburg/Berchtesgaden

—8 A.M. Hotel Kirschen, breakfast in artful dining room; musical instruments everywhere; classical music playing. Elegant presentation—fine linen. Owner, proper aristocrat, serves cornucopia of fruits, cheeses, breads.

—10:30. Sightseeing around Hoyensalzberg til noon. Pretty girl at river's edge selling ice cream says go to Berchtesgaden for mtn. scenery, beauty.

—1:30 train to Berchtesgaden via Freilassing. Eerie contrasts on landscape as train follows river into Alps; 3rd Reich images of WWII train movies. Think of Dad, the warrior, also Neville Chamberlain. Serpentine tracks along river; upward gaze to mythic human forms in towering rocks—Sleeping Witch, scary.

—Berchtesgaden Station, built by Albert Speer, earmarks of 3rd Reich, block-ish design. Curt stationmaster—unterfürher: sieg hail!

—initial disorientation—go to tourist bureau for info and bearings; catch bus to base of Jenner; chairlift to top; stunning panorama; create drawing showing lattice of paths skirting many mountain plateaus; cow bells ringing in distance, crystalline Konigsee below.

—3:00 hike down mtn.; come to hutte, finding festive Germans drinking heavenly beer, playing "oompah" music and singing; pass on into sub-alpine forest; realize may not make last train to Salzburg.

—5:00 hitchhike on road halfway down mtn, picked up by 2 German girls, Annemarie, Henrika.

—My "grace" T-shirt prompts discussion re. writing, spirit; AM takes me to bus station but we divert for short hike; pass along river feeling of synchrony, commonality; she is very natural, attractive, athletic; discussion about Killarney conference, monks, Buddhism. Wants to see me next day; heart skips beat.

—7 P.M. return to Salz. Hotel; grab pack; check into nearby hostel. Spinning fantasies about upcoming hike, connection with AM, Bavarian nature girl.

—10:30 turn in at hostel, exhausted.

You may note that my annotations and descriptions are of several types:

—*Mood and Atmosphere of Place*—scary Sleeping Witch in rocks; eerie Berchtesgaden landscape, crystalline Konigsee

—*People Characterizations*—AM, Bavarian nature girl; aristocratic proprietor; "unterfürher" stationmaster.

—*Realizations*—connections between Dad, the military man, and the warrior past of Berchtesgaden

—*Symbols*—Sleeping Witch in the Rocks above windy train tracks.

—*Dramas, Ironies, and Synchronicities*—the meeting with a German girl who shares my interest in spirit.

Although this was an unusually rich day and my descriptors are more elaborate than usual, the entry illustrates the process of sensory marking. Important events and meetings have been tagged with adjectives, symbols, and metaphors that promote retrieval and deeper probing. Each event, person, or place now stands for a packet of information that can be magnified for closer inspection. For example, I can retrieve the hotel proprietor and examine how his clothing, manner, and language suggest aristocratic bearing; I can examine aspects of Annemarie that are girl-like or nature-like; I can think more deeply and express more clearly what it is about Berchtesgaden that made me think of my father.

Barometric Ratings

Your barometric ratings are your daily ratings of health, emotional well-being, and creativity. In chapter 2, you set up your own rating system and benchmarks. Now is the time to apply them as you review how you felt over the course of the day. Here is my own example for

9/20/94. My ratings for that day are indicated by a checkmark. You might want to set up your journal so that all you have to do is circle the number that applies.

Physcial Condition Rating

Rating	Condition	Notes
√5	Excellent	Energetic, no allergies, back OK; no diet problem, indigestion
4	Good	
3	Fair	
2	Poor	
1	Terrible	

Emotional/Spiritual Condition Rating

Rating	Condition	Notes
√5	Excellent	Euphoric about meeting Annemarie
4	Good	
3	Fair	
2	Poor	
1	Terrible	

Creative Condition Rating

Rating	Condition	Notes
√5	Excellent	Lithe descriptions, good sketch from Jenner; ideas for a novel
4	Good	
3	Fair	
2	Poor	
1	Terrible	

If you have the time you might want to annotate your ratings as I have in column 3.

Mindset/Buddha Nature Rating

A shorthand method for evaluating mindset is to rate numerically the Buddha nature you practiced during a given day. You can do this by giving a number (or color-coding) to the various slices of the blank mandalas you have recorded in your daily log. Try to be consistent, giving the highest value of 5 to a dominant mindset and the practices associated with it. (If you have forgotten the elements of each credo and the perspective of each of the Buddhas, review the thumbnails in chapter 4.) I have exemplified this below for my day in Berchtesgaden.

Mandala of Your Buddha Nature

Train to Berchtesgaden; climb Jenner; meet AM while hitchhiking

Explorer

Enlightened Warrior

Conversation with German girls; deeper communication with AM

Thinker

5

Communicator

4

Healer

Harlequin

Mystic

3

Artist

Sketch of room in Salzburg; panorama sketch of top of Jenner

Accounting and Mechanics

Your daily record of expenditures summarizes expenses within specific categories which you compile each day. Below is the format I used on my last trip to Europe.

Date:

	Local currency	$US	Surplus/Deficit (see budget)	Notes
Lodging				
Food and Groceries				
Gifts				
Entertainment				
Books, Literature				
Transportation				
Dining/Meals				
Health				
Toiletries				
Other				
Routine Expenses				
Subtotal				
Total Day Expenses				

I always convert to dollars so that I can more easily relate expenditures in foreign currency to my budget. After I have made a daily entry I bring the total forward to my master expense table (see table 2–1), at which point I check to determine whether I am running at a surplus or deficit relative to my budget. If I have accumulated a sufficient reserve I might spend it on something special, for example, a night on the town with all of the Buddhas, a concert, or a gift for a friend.

As important as the expenditure log is the filing of receipts. I date and mark mine by type of expenditure and location, and then place them in a marked Ziploc bag.

Expression and Brainstorming

A journal without play is lifeless. My play includes madcap inventions, plots for movies and novels, letters, cartoons, thought-maps, and sketches. Most are recorded in the back of my journal.

Thought-Maps

Thought-maps are merely spontaneous graphics, usually combining text and drawings, in which you record uncensored thoughts and sensations. As the thoughts are committed to ink or pencil you begin making connections, probing commonalities, causality, and unifying symbols. This can be extremely valuable in clarifying intention, defining a travel plan, or solving a vexing problem while on the road.

You can initiate the process any way you like. It may begin with a key word, phrase, or image from something read or observed. Once I get started, I give myself license to go sideways, backwards and forwards, and to pop up and down to different levels. I switch spontaneously from writing to drawing. I never erase. The idea is to value all thought and invite free expression, association, and discharge. The thought-map from my 1994 trip to Europe represents spontaneous reflections on several problems and questions I was considering while in transit to France—whether to rendezvous with Annemarie in Nice, how various experiences and ideas might be expressed in a novel I would call "Ten of Hearts," and whether it was time to return home. The main questions and solutions are represented in the interconnected spheres. The circle in the upper right details ideas and books which I could draw on to answer my questions.

If I have been thinking about a problem and considering options I may spin out images that I associate with different alternatives. I like to think dramatically and express whatever symbols come to mind. Throughout the process I test myself to make associations and connections. How does one event or idea link to another? What are the unifying symbols and ideas?

Another way to proceed is to invite each of the Buddhas to sound off. You never know what will occur. Healer may go off on a tangent about mind-body interaction and that might bring up thoughts from Deepak Chopra or Candace Pert, and then Artist might take over, spinning out caricatures of people on the road. This in turn could provoke an image of an Indian guru, and then suddenly the issue could become spiritual touchstones and how they relate to the latest adventure.

All this would simply be discharge but for the fact that at least a few thoughts and linkages always deserve deeper probing. Sometimes I do this in Step 8.

Sketches

Sketches can be extremely grounding and insight-provoking if you aren't too hard on yourself about your limitations as an artist.

The first thing that happens when you try to render something is that you are forced to study it closely. You soon discover lines, shapes, texture, and form that you were previously unaware of. Next time you go to a museum, instead of joining the cattle rush from one painting to the next, stop and try to render one of the masterpieces, if only in colored pencil. Try your hand at a Van Gogh, Escher, or Renoir. You may fail miserably (in your own eyes) but you will be sensitized to the skill of the artist and the problems that he or she grappled with.

As a result, your consciousness will change. Art and the subjects of the art will affect you differently. You will never look at a vineyard in quite the same way after trying to re-create one by Van Gogh. And after trying your hand at an Escher waterwheel, every stream or waterwheel will present a test of your ability to make water run uphill. Maybe most important of all, you will began applying an artistic mentality to problems and situations where perhaps in the past you relied exclusively on rational/logical skills. As described in chapter 4, different questions and curiosities will come to you, and you will fix on novel and innovative possibilities that might otherwise seem outlandish.

Step 8. Deeper Probing of Daily Dramas

The purpose of the deeper probing step is to review progress in meeting objectives, uncover developing dramas, and look for the presence or absence of Buddha nature.

Review of Objectives and Footprints on the Path

At the end of the week, and sometimes more often, I review my daily entries to monitor thought and action relative to my intentions, objectives, and strategy. Rather than concentrate on outcomes, I focus on the mindset I am practicing and the dramas I am playing out.

As reflected in my own travel intentions and objectives, what usually matters most to me are joy, sense of freedom, intellectual stimulation, people connections, artistic expression, and mystical experience. My daily log always gives me a pretty good indication of whether this is what I am realizing.

Finding and Writing the Drama

If you can find and express the dramas you are caught up in, you heighten the potential for escaping what is unwanted and realizing your most heartfelt intentions. Although I sometimes express these dramas in my drawings, my main vehicle is letter writing to myself and friends.

I rely on two basic writing techniques—zooming-in and zooming-out. In zooming-in you identify fully with an event or experience, almost reliving it as you record what has happened to you. The process is visceral, emotional, and sensory. You don't try to be objective. Like a good novelist writing in first person, you are at one with your characters and the emphasis is on feeling. No one exemplifies this better than Henry Miller.

Zooming-In

Description of Kenneth Patchen by Henry Miller

A sort of sincere assassin, I thought to myself, as we shook hands. This impression never left me . . . He is a fizzing human bomb ever threatening to explode in our midst. Tender and ruthless at the same time, he has the faculty of strangling the very ones who wish to help him. He is inexorable; he has no manner, no tact, no grace. He gives no quarter. Like the gangster, he follows a code of his own. He gives you a chance to put up your hands before shooting you down. Most people however, are too terrified to throw up their hands. They get mowed down.

This is the monstrous side of him, which makes him appear ruthless and rapacious. Within the snorting dragon, however, there is a gentle prince who suffers at the mention of the slightest cruelty or injustice. A tender soul, who soon learned to envelope himself in a mantle of fire in order to protect his sensitive skin. . . .

The limitation of zooming-in is that you often miss the bigger picture and you are often caught up in ego and judgment. For this reason it is usually valuable to alternate your close-up view with a long-range view—panning to a more distant perspective and inviting your Buddhas (particularly Harlequin) to make some objective sense of impression.

In zooming-out (or panning) you look for gestalt and over-arching themes. In effect, you ask yourself: What are the patterns I have been caught up in? What are the conflicts? What forces are at work on this terrain? What are the interpersonal dynamics that account for what is happening to me? What is going on at different levels—physical, emotional, creative, and spiritual? What inertia is present and what seems to be headed for a dramatic resolution? What are my avenues of escape and transcendence?

The switch is from the near to the far, from the subjective to the objective, from the personal to the detached. Zooming-in enables you to feel and express more deeply, while zooming-out invokes panorama and essence. This mixed technique is particularly valuable if you are trying to rebalance or troubleshoot (Step 9). It is also beneficial at the end of a trip when you are trying to bring lessons home (Step 10).

8

Sensory Delights of Mindful Travel

Mindful travel awakens the senses. Colors are more vibrant and electric; sound is brighter and stirs an inner song; images race across our inner screens as we sense we are part of an unfolding drama.

Attention and space are the main requirements—give your attention to the present moment and separate yourself from the discordant, frictional spinning of a runaway mind. Breathe out vexation and anxiety and inhale the clean, untainted air. Allow it to work its way through the bloodstream. It will find the hidden pathways and revitalize them. Like holy water passing down a stream, it will cleanse and renew, second by second finding its way to the deep pools where Buddha as Mystic is ready to create his magic.

> *As you walk and eat and travel, be where you are. Otherwise you will miss most of your life.*
> -BUDDHA
>
> *Everything in the world comes from the mind, like objects appearing from the sleeve of a magician.*
> -LANKAVATAR SUTRA

As the writer John Welwood states, "Life has its own sacredness, which shines most brightly when we get out of the way." This is the imperative—eliminate the blockages and impediments; obliterate the dams that keep the life force from coursing through us. When we are on the road, this often seems easier. It is easier for us to let go and breathe. It is easier to hold that breath and let it stir our sleeping Buddha nature.

Journeys to Sacred Places

"Where is Buddha to be found?" asks the student of the Zen master.

"Go scrub the floor," answers the master.

The missing Buddha may be found in the strangest places. Devoted disciples go on far-flung pilgrimages to find him, journeying to Lourdes, Mecca, Jerusalem, and Angkor Wat. They cluster under the Bodhi Tree and they wade into the opaque waters of the Ganges at Benares. Vast sums are spent by pilgrims to deepen their faith and strengthen their convictions.

Not all the sacred places are mapped and marked. Not all are described in sacred texts, but somehow we feel their pull when they are near.

Thoreau experienced this at Walden Pond, John Muir in the wildlands of the West and among the great Sequoias. For the artist Georgia O'Keeffe it was the desert Southwest where old bones bleach in the sun, and for the poet May Sarton, the forested seashore of New England.

Whatever our Mecca or Shambhala, it is always the place that quiets our storms and makes us feel whole. Sometimes it is the home of our ancestors, for others places we associate with freedom or an identity yet unrealized.

Paris was such a place for the writer Henry Miller. Living in poverty in New York during the 1920s, he dreamed of an escape to Paris, where surrounded by avant-garde artists, émigré intellectuals, film-makers, and musicians, he might begin a career as a writer. Arriving overseas in his thirty-third year, he was alive with energy and ready to bring about his new life, no matter what the sacrifice. It didn't take long for Paris to help him find his voice.

> It is now the fall of my second year in Paris. I have been sent here for a reason, I have not yet been able to fathom.
> I have no money, no resources, no hopes. I am the happiest man alive. A year ago, six months ago, I thought that I was an artist. I no longer think about it, I am.

Later in life he would relive the early feelings of those years in Paris and reflect on how the streets of Paris fortified him:

> Walking with my friend through the deserted streets I was reliving my first days in Paris, for it was in the Rue de Vanves that my new life really began. Night after night without money, without friends, without a language I had walked these streets in despair and anguish. The streets were everything to me, as they must be to every man who is lost in a big city. Walking through them again with my countryman I congratulated myself silently that I had begun my life in Paris behind the scenes, as it were. . . . Like it or not, I was obliged to create a new life for myself. And this new life I feel is mine, absolutely mine, to use or to smash, as I see fit. In this life I am god, and like god I am indifferent to my own fate. I am everything there is—so why worry?

A feeling of immanent grace is present in sacred places. The words of "Amazing Grace" apply: "I once was lost but now I'm found; was blind but now I see." Not only do we feel more grounded, but senses quicken. Vision may actually improve—not only our ability to discern form and color, but the ability of the mind's eye to see what we must do and where we must go to make ourselves whole. So often the experience of travel sends us down a path with more heart and meaning.

There is also a feeling of embodiment. So often the rat race of modern life makes us feel empty and outside ourselves. At home we may be numbed by our obligations and sense of entrapment. At work we may feel diminished by organizational hierarchies that pigeonhole us. All doors seem shut; all paths gated and closed. We dare not try anything new or we are sure to be slammed, rejected, and rebuked. If our mates don't leave us for our petulance, our children will laugh at us. If we try to break out of a professional rut we will endanger our retirement, which is the one shred of potential freedom we still cling to.

Our bodies reflect the restricted freedom, whether the symptoms are shallow breathing, chronic aches and pains, or weakened immune systems.

When we find a sacred place it is common for breathing to deepen, muscles to relax, feeling to return to numbed limbs. Our *chi* or life force begins to pulse and our occluded inner pathways flow with energy. Maybe for the first time since youth, we feel that what we do matters. We are part of a larger whole and can make a significant contribution. This in turn deepens our breathing and even more of our armor crumbles. No doubt this is one of the reasons why so many spontaneous healings occur at Lourdes and other sacred places.

The sacred place for one of my travel friends was a mysterious paradise in the eastern Alps he called Kafiristan. He named it after the Himalayan refuge in Kipling's short story, *The Man Who Would Be King.* Supposedly it was surrounded by an inland sea and curtained by needlelike spires that repelled northern invaders. The spires were sculpted by wind and rain into mythological figures that in certain light seemed to grin mischievously, as if in sole possession of the answer to a great cosmic riddle.

"Kafiristan" by Jim Currie.

Fortified by beer, my friend would insist that his Kafiristan was founded by the Cathars who had been driven out of southern France during the Albignesian inquisition and diaspora (ca. 1350 A.D.). Finding their way to the Dolomites they created a secret gnostic civilization that lasted several hundred years. It eventually crumbled but the spirits of the master monks remained in the rocks and ruins.

I was so taken by this story that I decided to try my hand at a drawing of Kafiristan. Kafiristan is now my own inner refuge when I meditate or feel the need for solitary reflection.

Travels in an Archaic Land

Traveling with openness and awareness works a strange effect on inner navigation. We enter a field of possibility that reverses our polarities. Compass needles quicken; divining rods twitch. We know better than to relax as we sense the eruption of something important and defining. These were my sensations in 1994 when I traveled by train to Berchtesgaden.

Just outside of Bad Reichenhall, the valley began to narrow and the mountains steepen, forming craggy faces where heaven meets earth. Storm clouds huddled ominously at the nexus like a charged ether, infusing each stony visage with lifeblood. A sentinel extruding from the mountain wall commanded my attention. He was inspecting us closely, apparently deciding whether we were interlopers, and if so whether we were cause for alarm. A shrug in the talus caused scree to run down the lower slope next to the grade, and for a moment I wondered if the train would be buried in a raging slide. To my relief, the rock-fall abated. Apparently we were no real threat. The train continued on, paralleling the serpentine path of a frothing river.

With every kilometer the landscape grew more wild and furious. The river and mountains seemed to be at war, and for the moment the mountains were ascendant, constricting flow through a narrow, bouldered channel. The river foamed with intemperance and then fell into a deep gorge, roaring like a maimed stag.

I wondered what sensations Neville Chamberlain felt and thought when he came here by train from Munich in 1938 to negotiate with Hitler in Obersalzberg. He, too, must have been struck by the dark immanence of the Bavarian Alps and this place, in particular. Maybe it even occurred to him that he was out of his element.

This was stark contrast to the tame flatlands of the English wolds. This was a geography of Id and impulse, intuition and emotion. Detached reason could hardly be sustained in a place like this. You might easily wonder whether deep within these mountains was the dark eruptive core of a German *zeitgeist—a zeitgeist* and destiny it was futile to resist.

Hitler had written about this plot of ground in *Mein Kampf,* pouring out a conviction that here powerful shadow forces were stirring that would impel the Third Reich to rise up from betrayal and humiliation and recapitulate the glory of Charlemagne.

I wondered how my friend Camarano might square all this with his "dramatic imperative." Perhaps he would say something to the effect that Hitler was simply projecting his own demented inner turmoil onto the landscape and then drawing upon the petulant skies and wizened faces in the rocks to rationalize his own nightmarish fantasies. And yet Camarano did tell me to look for the "fairies" at different sites in the Alps. The fairies were supposed to inspirit his mythical Kafiristan.

Yes, he seemed to believe that different places possessed unique energies and these energies could be strong enough to affect thought and consciousness. Maybe they even acted as magnets for people to play out their own dramatic imperatives.

The weather was taking a severe turn. The train passed into a forbidding shadow and summer rain pelted the windows angrily. It stopped as quickly as it started, causing the train to be cloaked in a steamy veil. We passed around another bend and were struck by radiant sunshine. All around me color burst forth from the shadows—raw umber in the foliage, vermilion and magenta in the storm-laden clouds. The play of light reminded me of the moody contrasts of Breughel and Vermeer. (Jim Currie, "Ten of Hearts," unpublished manuscript)

Indulgence—Taking the Deeper Drink

On occasion you come to a place where you need to indulge, a place to take a deeper drink and maybe linger and loiter until you are staggering from fatigue. If it is an Irish pub, you buy drinks for the house and allow your feet to tattoo the floor with jig rhythms. If it is a Paris cafe, you feast on the color and bustle of the street and spend an afternoon writing letters to friends. If it is a high mountain perch, you inhale the perfume of wildflowers and test your singing voice.

One of my dearest friends, a vibrant woman known to family and friends as Gigi, found such a place in Hartz Mountain in the North Cascades. In her youth she dreamed of becoming a New York stage actress and singer, but abandoned that during the Depression for the security of marriage. Though she found outlets for her creativity, she ceased her singing.

At age sixty, she traveled to Hartz Mountain on a hiking and camping trip. There, surrounded by larks and jays, inhaling the crisp mountain air, she began to sing again. At first her fledgling notes were weak and uncertain, but she kept at it and eventually she was soaring, singing the way she had in her youth. Hartz Mountain is now a place she comes to often to commune with the birds and sing to her heart's delight.

Another artist friend named Andrea sings in her own way in fishing villages. Nothing makes her feel so alive as to be surrounded by decaying wooden boats, gulls screaming ravenously above an incoming trawler, and fishermen in yellow slickers casting off to the open sea. She can spend twelve hours straight at the end of a pier filling a notebook with luminous watercolors.

I have the same weakness for fishing villages, especially those of Brittany and Ireland, but a close second are train stations. I never mind missing a train, especially when I am armed with a Eurail Pass that entitles me to unlimited travel. I also enjoy simply meandering through a bustling station, watching the constant arrival and departure of trains, and listening attentively to the mellifluous announcements coming over the PA system. The pleasure only intensifies if I am in Paris and the voice is that of a French mademoiselle announcing sensuously, "Attention, Mesdames and Monsieurs, the TGV pour Quimper part à quai trois, voie quatre." And then comes that defining single bell-tone declaring that the precious moment is hand. I close my eyes and breathe deeply, overcome with ecstasy.

Sight and Brush-Stroke

I wouldn't think of going on a long-distance trip without colored pencils and a few pastels for drawings. Sights and scenes that others take photographs of I stop to draw. A sketch or drawing slows you down and forces you to study what lies before you. In the process you begin to see light, color, and shadow in a different way. You discover that each sunset is layered with clouds that play a teasing game with the sun. Each passing cloud creates a mask, and yet never is the mask completely impermeable. Sometimes just enough light filters through to create a glistening diaphanous veil. A photograph is a freeze-frame; a drawing is a study of change, including the waves of emotion you feel as you render something. If you simply don't have time to make a sketch, go ahead and take a photograph, but when you do, consider composition, changing light and shadows, and the feelings that these evoke.

As artist you look at a rose in a different way. Each petal, you discover, is a unique teardrop with a different hue and shape than the others. Look more closely and you see a drama in progress—aphids serrating a smooth edge or creating a window that illuminates an inner vault.

Sometimes the drawings come easily; other times they are labored and feeble. With no shame whatsoever I will take my sketch pad to the Musée d'Orsay, the Louvre, and other famous galleries and museums. Surrounded by a crowd, I remove my implements and begin sketching a famous Renoir, Klee, Magritte, or Picasso.

Within a few minutes I sense spies and gawkers. One or two people will be looking over my shoulder at my masterpiece in progress. I will play the role of professional artist, scribbling with more vitality and recklessness, disdaining subdued pastels for wild reds, moody magenta, and recriminating shades of violet. After all, what counts is the spirit of the act—the *jeu d'esprit.*

Incredibly more than a few of these drawings turn out to be pretty interesting. They never look very much like the originals but usually possess style and originality.

One of the great curiosities of art is its subjectivity and individuality. No two artists worth their salt could ever replicate the work of another. Monet's water lilies at Giverney would never look like Manet's, and neither artist could re-create Van Gogh's vineyards in Provence. It's not a matter of technique; they couldn't do it because they don't see in the same way. A water lily is never just color and form in a particular light, but a packet of sensation and thought that no camera can ever capture.

Mind is always at work and distorts in its own way to see more clearly.

Never is this so clear as in viewing Van Gogh's Provence on a journey by train from Marseilles to Nantes. The natural landscape is serene and becalmed. Colors are bleached, almost bloodless: diluted orange roofs, bleached-clay buildings, light-pastel foliage. Only a very strange and wizened genius could find tension in such a place. And yet this is exactly what Van Gogh accomplishes with his oils, in part by reaching for a palette knife rather than a brush. As a result, even the softest forms are roiled with emotion. Vincent is testament to the fact that one person's becalmed sea is another's raging deluge.

Giving yourself up to Buddha as Artist, you never know whether a composition will work but you can be confident that your effort will offer some kind of lesson. One of my most glorious failures (which I repeat every time I go to Paris) is a rendering of the Hôtel de Ville on the Right Bank across from Île de la Cité. Though my skills as an artist have probably trebled in the last ten years, I am always humbled by this ornate gingerbread edifice and its elaborate terra cotta vaults, ledges, and grotesques.

Try as I may, Hôtel de Ville always eludes me. Why I am not exactly sure—perhaps mental imbalance or sacrilege in a previous life. I do know that it presents the cardinal problem in art—balancing detail and essence. If I reach for the broad-brush and ignore the detail, I create a face without a personality. And yet if I succumb to detail, tracking the endless lines and interconnecting planes, my drawing devolves into jumble. As if these challenges weren't enough, the moving sun complicates everything by changing shadows and highlights.

Every one of my drawings is a wretched debacle. And yet in each struggle I learn something about the perennial problem of finding the equable balance between detail and essence, foreground and background. I can now render larger pieces of the whole, even though the gestalt is still missing.

I am convinced that if a decent drawing eventually emerges, it will be because I have managed an elusive stillness in my own anxious mind. In that precious moment of serenity, the sun will freeze, time will stop, and the essence of Hôtel de Ville will arise in a soft vapor. I will be close to the omega point often described in religious/philosophical writing that arrives in a perfect egoless communion with God.

9
Solving Problems on the Road

Step 9. Troubleshooting and Rebalancing

In your preparations before departure, you considered what might go wrong and developed a strategy with contingency plans. Hopefully this is helping you deal with the predictable snafus and impediments of travel. As you work through each individual problem, be aware that mindset and attitude are critical elements of any solution.

> *Yield and overcome; bend and be straight; empty and be full; wear out and be new; have little and gain; have much and be confused.*
>
> -LAO-TZU

There is always the temptation to give someone a piece of your mind who fouls up your reservations or frustrates you, but it seldom helps and most often takes a toll by contracting spirit. An occasional flare-up is to be expected, but if you don't soon breathe it away you risk the loss of your higher powers, including creativity, rationality, healing capabilities, and communication skills. These are always more important than the false satisfaction that comes from lashing out or cursing the darkness.

Step 9a. Troubleshooting

In your travel strategy you may have accounted for a variety of snafus, including the following:

- potential friction with a spouse or travel companion
- health breakdowns
- loss of important documents
- theft or victimization
- loss of money or credit cards
- sexual harassment
- problems staying warm or dry

In the turmoil of the moment it is easy to forget the sensible well-considered steps you already defined for the problem at hand. Go back and review them and also the mindset you wanted to bring to your trip.

Here are some additional tips for problems that might not be fully covered by your strategies:

1. Not Getting Along with Spouse or Mate

As described in chapter 6, whenever people take on partners, tacit systems are set up for solving problems. These relate to shared and joint responsibility—who is to gather information, who is to come up with options, who makes a final decision, how each partner can appeal if the other person appears to be out of their bloody mind.

Quite often when you aren't getting along with your mate the real argument isn't happening—you are arguing about something secondary to the real issue. Although the surface issue may be inattentive driving, exchanging money, getting lost, or the blow-up of a lodging arrangement, the real and underlying issue may be the conventions for decision-making that leaves one person out in the cold.

When friction persists about the small things, try to pop up to a higher level. Ask your partner if some discussion is needed about the way you as a team are making decisions. Ask whether it is possible to make some adjustments so that each of you might be able to meet your needs. Try to be clear on what those needs are. If you have done your advance work, you should have a pretty good idea, not only of what you want to see, visit, and do, but the way you want to approach each experience and feel about it.

Consider the possibility of splitting up for awhile. Time spent apart may give each of you the opportunity to explore in your own way. Often this is a tonic to a relationship: when you get back together with a mate, you are both energized and feel individually validated. Hopefully you have the kind of relationship that will allow for such independence.

You may be surprised to discover that many of the original assumptions you made about the interests of your partner are off-base. This happens frequently when one person develops the travel plan and the other is not consulted. If on the road you discover such a lack of connection, go back and together look at the questions in chapter 6 dealing with travel partners. You might also want to review the discussion of travel objectives in chapter 5.

Be aware of the fact that it isn't easy to change conventions and strategies in midstream, especially when time is limited. Travelmates who can't meet or reach an accommodation ought to consider going their separate ways.

2. Not Able to Escape Thoughts of Problems Back Home

If you find yourself unable to leave problems behind as I did in 1998, reevaluate your intentions and objectives. Perhaps you need a course change. Your inner intentions are going to affect, if not control, your attention and your energy, so there is no point in trying to force yourself to stick with a plan that is at odds with what you are really looking for.

In thinking about this, enlist Buddha as Thinker to consider ways to alter the basic strategy to take best advantage of the time that remains. Quite often only small changes are necessary to accommodate your needs. You may decide to go to the same places, but simply spend your time differently.

If the chatter and noise persist, it may be time for discharge. My most reliable standby is vigorous exercise. You may think you are already exercising by carrying around luggage or a pack, but vigorous exercise is different. It energizes and cleanses rather than fatigues. It speeds up your breathing and metabolism and releases calming chemicals throughout your body. I find that exercise followed by meditation is particularly powerful.

Another option is the Rx of insomniacs—painting the blackest possible picture of what lies ahead. Take your worries to the hilt. The full monty. If your job is the issue, assume you are going to be discredited and fired. Imagine a doomsday scenario with all the trappings—total repudiation, embarrassment, and humiliation. Picture yourself as George Costanza when his employer walked in on him when he was napping under his desk or discovered that he was committing indiscretions with the cleaning lady. If possible find a copy of Henry Miller's novel, *Tropic of Cancer,* and recite the following cheery passage:

There will be more calamities, more death, more despair. Not the slightest indication of a change anywhere. The cancer of time is eating us away. Our heroes have killed themselves or are killing themselves. The hero then, is not time but timelessness. We must get in step, a lock step, toward the prison of death. There is no escape. The weather will not change.

There is nothing quite so therapeutic as a good vent, but it must be unmitigated—the full funeral dirge, the kiss of death, and the surrender to pitch-black darkness. It is in the coldness of the complete nuclear shadow that renewal begins as it did for Henry Miller.

3. Love at First Sight—Through Rose-Colored Glasses

Travel romances hold great allure for almost everyone. In a strange and exotic place we feel less inhibited and more free. We open ourselves up to others and they do the same. This can be wonderful and disastrous and often wonderfully disastrous.

Young people are especially prone to flings, most often with other travelers, but people of all ages leap without thinking too much about the practical consequences. It is as if we have all been transformed into Don Quixote, rosily distorting our surroundings and surrendering to romantic illusions.

On my own trip to Berchtesgaden I managed to convince myself in less than three days that I was in love with Annemarie. (I must have been narcotized by the clean pure air of the high Alps, the breathtaking scenery, and the star-struck circumstances of our meeting.)

Away from my home, unencumbered by the need to get up and go to work, to think about commitments to my elderly parents, I was ready to invest myself in this relationship, and possibly move to Berchtesgaden. No problem seemed insurmountable. Ignore the fact that I spoke no German, had no solid prospects for work, lacked substantial savings, and really knew nothing about Annemarie. Ignore the fact that when Annemarie and I weren't passionately embracing, we were agitating each other like dancing scorpions. Distortion abounded. I was hardly practicing Buddha nature. If Buddha was involved at all, he was upside down, dizzily looking at the world between his legs.

Fortunately my brain wasn't so addled that I didn't realize that I needed some time on my own. A voice came to me, not unlike that of Sancho Panza, telling me that I needed some separation. I caught a train to Munich and while working on my journal realized the crazy drama that I was playing out. Obviously Annemarie and I needed a candid talk, and if we wanted to deepen our relationship we probably ought to arrange for some time together away from Berchtesgaden. Perhaps we should try traveling together or I should invite her to visit me in the States.

On my return to Berchtesgaden I tried to corner her for a heart-to-heart talk but she saw no need to talk. A favorite band was playing at a local beer garden and she wanted to dance. There, while staring into her seductive eyes, it occurred to me that we were equally stubborn and willful; she wouldn't be happy until she tamed me and most probably would decide along the way that she needed a greater challenge. This relationship was nitroglycerine and the imminent explosion would likely immolate all sixteen Buddhas (hers and mine) simultaneously. In a few days the pyrotechnics started again and I streaked for the train station before the grand flash.

The two of us remained in touch after my return to the States, and from afar managed some light teasing and torture until finally both of us came to our senses and ended it.

The relationship, however, had a ripple effect. I related the story to a writer friend from Princeton, who is even more prone to travel romance than I, and he broke into delirious laughter. He understood exactly what I had experienced, as he too had been involved with stubborn and exotic foreign women while living in Nuremberg. One woman in particular had captivated him—a beautiful Hungarian, not unlike my Annemarie. The relationship had fallen apart and she had returned to Budapest. That was ten years ago.

Suddenly he surprised me by declaring that perhaps it was time to call her back and see how the years had been treating her. I sensed trouble but said nothing. A month later I learned that the two of them had been corresponding and were talking about a rendezvous. Three weeks after that he announced that they had discovered a deep spiritual connection and he was flying to Budapest.

"Just for an exploratory visit?" I asked.

"No," he replied, "to see if we can make a life together." He was deadly serious. He had already shed most of his possessions and said goodbye to Mom, Dad, and his siblings. Once in Budapest his true love would find him a job. He was quick to add that Budapest was an exciting, progressive city and he was sure he could acclimate to the culture.

"Budapest?" I replied curiously.

"Yes," he assured me.

I wished him well and bit my lip as three of my Buddhas cried out for me to slap him back to his senses.

Four weeks later he rang me up on the phone. I assumed he was in Budapest. "How is it going?" I burst forth. "There's got to be a terrific story here."

"More than you could imagine," he answered ruefully. "It started at the airport."

First, his true love had ballooned a bit since he had seen her last.

She was also a bit more rigid than he remembered. "Fossilized rigidity, you might say, which apparently is *de rigueur* for the Hungarian princess."

"This sounds awful. How about the royal family?"

"Ah yes, Mom and Dad. They were there waiting for me at the airport in the family armor. Mace, lances, and vats of boiling oil."

"To prevent the kidnapping of the beloved daughter to Americay?"

"Exactly."

"Well, what are you going to do?"

"It's already done. I'm home."

"Home where?"

"Here, Seattle. And by the way, it's Shangri-La compared to Budapest. The smoking almost killed me. What was I thinking?"

4. Persistent or Acute Health Problems

In your advance preparation you may have identified specific sensitivities as well as steps to take when you come down with a cold or flu or something more serious. If you do run into problems, remember that you may only be a phone call away from help. Don't be reluctant to place a long-distance phone call to your doctor back home who should be able to fax you a prescription or offer an idea that you may have overlooked.

In northern Europe you will also find a wealth of good health advice available in health food stores and naturopathic apothecaries. Remember also that you can access the web at most local libraries. The International Society of Travel Medicine at www.istm.org that I mentioned above will give you names and numbers of local English-speaking doctors.

A Eurail Pass can also be invaluable if you feel the onset of a cold or the flu. On several occasions this has been my trip-saver. With the arrival of sniffles and a scratchy throat I headed for the nearest station and caught a train for the Riviera or Côte d'Azur. There the Mediterranean sun worked its magic and nursed me back to health.

5. No People Connections or the Wrong Breed of Cat

It is important to recognize people who feed your spirit, those who weaken it, and those who are the wrong stripe to travel with. Unless you are a venerable Tibetan *tulku* or *rinpoche* and decide that your trip is simply an exercise in service and compassion, pay attention to the outlook, mindset, and interests of potential travelmates.

Remember that if you have signed up with a spouse or mate (boyfriend or girlfriend), you are limited in your ability to disconnect and follow your own path. Solo travelers can usually meet people along the way to share experiences and costs and gain security in numbers.

Exercise Discrimination in Short-Term Partners

If you do travel solo and you do decide to take on a short-term partner, exercise discrimination, considering not only safety and commonality of interests but basic mindset. My own experiences in this area are checkered. When I am on the road I tend to see most everyone in a positive light. If someone suggests that we travel together I am usually quick to oblige, and usually after a day or so grow restive, realizing that our intentions are different, our values are realms apart, and our travel rhythms at variance. I then have to confront the disharmony and disengage.

It is never easy to say goodbye to someone, and it particularly difficult when you have to tell them why in nonjudgmental fashion. Of course, this itself can be taken as a valuable challenge. I find that parting is always less traumatic and painful when it is governed by clarity of intention and self-awareness. This is why your journal, including written intentions, touchstones, an inventory, and a daily log, is so useful. It serves to remind you of who you are and what your journey is about. As a result, you are empowered to follow your own higher truth and cut the ties that hold you back.

"It's not you; it's me."

Don't Be Too Quick to Judge

When you are on the look-out for interesting people to talk to, avoid premature judgments based on looks, age, clothing, and so forth. Even the most enlightened souls frequently prejudge people based upon looks or manner. Passing through Liechtenstein, I shared a train compartment with a dowdy, middle-aged woman who was knitting. I couldn't imagine that we had anything to talk about until I noticed a book by Rudolf Steiner peaking out at me beneath her balls of yarn. This provoked my curiosity and before long she was offering a Jungian perspective on why people stay stuck and why they change. She was quick to add her own insights. Apparently she was a prominent psychologist who had been trained in Zurich. For three hours we talked in freshets about our favorite authors and how we brought their ideas to our own lives. When she disembarked, she invited me to stay with her family in the Liechtenstein Alps.

Look for People in the Right Habitat

If you are still having difficulty making connections you might want to reexamine where you have been staying and whether it is isolating you. Hotels, especially stuffy expensive hotels, often attract stuffy people interested primarily in privacy. The layout of the hotel can also determine how people interact. A cold and unappealing lobby will send people directly to their rooms or perhaps a smoky bar.

Even when staying in hotels you can often make interesting connections if you engage people on their own terms. One thing is certain—if you go directly to your room when you arrive and only reappear at check-out, you cut yourself off from such opportunity.

Because most European hotels include breakfast in the fare, you can often connect with people mornings in a dining room. I generally find that this is a time when people like to extend themselves and are most open to conversation. Sometimes all it takes is eye contact and they will ask where you are headed.

At the other end of the spectrum of cost and privacy, hostels offer opportunities to connect with others; people are preselected to be sociable.

Favorite discussion topics include travel tips and cultural differences between countries. It never takes very long to get to know someone in a hostel even when you may not speak the same language.

In 1998 I stayed in a nondescript hostel in the gray Brittany town of Brest. I expected no more than shelter from the rainy weather. No one in the hostel seemed to speak English. Undaunted, I made a garbled attempt to socialize with the French woman running the hostel. She was very warm and engaging and surprised me by an invitation to dinner with several of her Breton friends. The meal included a variety of local delicacies, sampled during discussion about provincial culture, including dance, legend, and song.

A main disadvantage of hostels is unruly teenagers. On school vacations they make a night in a bunkroom unbearable, even when your ears are plugged or your Walkman is cranked. I make a point of staying abreast of vacation dates and when the time arrives detour to a cheap hotel, *pension,* or bed and breakfast.

Bed-and-breakfast inns are hard to peg. Opportunities to socialize are variable but usually greater than in hotels and somewhat less than in hostels. Defining variables include layout, price range, location, who happens to be there at the moment, and the general conviviality of the host or hostess.

Engage People on Their Own Terms

Whenever I feel alone or isolated I'll drop into a local pub. In most of Europe they attract a cross-section of the population and are a favorite spot for people to socialize and get to know one another. I particularly enjoy pubs in university towns like Oxford, Cambridge, and Heidelberg, where people gather to philosophize, brainstorm, and debate. In a Cambridge pub dating back to 1300, I met two young

German physicists open and willing to discuss their work. We were soon engaged in stirring conversation about T.S. Kuhn's *Structure of Scientific Revolutions,* and the social conditions that lead to scientific breakthroughs. I interjected that this was required reading in a college class I had taken from James Watson (who with Francis Crick discovered the structure of DNA).

One of them asked if Watson's reputation for playfulness was deserved and I passed on a few fifteen-year-old rumors to the effect that it was. The other German was quick to add that Watson's partner, Francis Crick was still here in Cambridge. In fact, Crick's lab, where much of the work on the double helix had occurred, was just across from his own. After we finished our beer I was treated to a late-night tour of the building.

In Ireland, you need only spring for a round of Guinness and the world instantly opens up to you. My first experience with this came in 1979, when I visited a famous fiddler's pub in the town of Doolin.

Cold and wet from hitchhiking in monsoon weather, I entered the pub and headed directly for the nearest fireplace. In front of it six or seven middle-aged musicians were tuning up their fiddles, guitars, mandolins, and banjos. I reached for my wallet and ordered a round of Guinness. With much-appreciated grog drooling from his lips, one of the fiddlers cleared an honored place for me at the twelve o'clock position in the circle of musicians. Two Irishmen to my right were playing fiddle; two on my left were working away on flute and mandolin. My job, they made clear, was to keep everyone well lubricated. I don't think I ever heard such lively music, and I took my responsibility for keeping it going very seriously.

Very late that night after I had downed more than my share of Ireland's finest, a toothless bear of a whistle player named Micho announced that he would put me up for the night. I was much relieved, as I knew I was in no condition to find a place to stay, especially at that late hour. He declared that I should "take care of the fire-starter" and meet him at the front door. I dutifully handed over several dollars to the barkeeper, not exactly sure what I was paying for.

A few minutes later I passed through the doorway into a ferocious storm. Micho was up ahead charging into the driving rain, not bothering to see if I was keeping up. Even if I had been more clear-headed, it wouldn't have been easy. We were following a narrow vertical path to the top of the cliffs above Doolin. (I subsequently learned that these were the storied cliffs of Moher that had repulsed Norse invaders and inspired Irish legends about shipwrecked sailors, protective fairies, and suicidal maidens.)

The seaward side of the path was preciously close to the edge. Below I could hear the thunderclap of breakers crashing into the rocks. If I didn't collect my wits, I'd soon be joining them.

We entered a dense meadow and Micho turned back toward me. "You've got the fire-starter, right?"

"The what? I thought you were picking it up."

"Jaysus!" he bellowed angrily. Not waiting for my reply, he surged into the storm at double-time. I started to turn back down the path but quickly reconsidered—one stumble and a new myth would be born about the American fool who forgot Micho's fire-starter and paid dearly for it.

No, I'd be better off following the bear-man and hoping his anger would abate. I rushed to catch up and in the process caught an image of myself weak and vulnerable. I was in trouble and no Buddha nature or invisible hand of God was likely to bail me out of this predicament.

Out of nowhere appeared a sod cottage nestled in a swale protected from the wind. Micho barged through the door but left it open. Apparently he knew I was still behind him. Like an obsequious mouse, I slipped inside, smiled meekly, and burped.

"You take the bed over there," he ordered, muttering how damnably cold it would be in the morning.

I fell quickly to sleep beneath a downy comforter and slept like a fatted sheep.

Around dawn I awakened to the cry of ravenous gulls riding updrafts above the cliffs. Micho was still asleep and snoring like a Celtic giant. I stepped lightly to the door and passed outside into a lush swale of wildflowers. A radiant fog had descended on the cottage, suffusing the wildflowers with a sparkling mist. My footprints glistened in a fine angel dust, and everywhere were cobwebs that seemed to be capturing some kind of enchantment. If Ireland were at once an island of uncertain commitment to reality, I seemed to have found the portal to that older dream world here in the Burren of County Clare.

A waterfall-like roar drew me to the other end of the swale. I came to a ledge and gazed below at towering breakers wasting themselves against the Cliffs of Moher. With each stroke of the sea, the waves exploded into sun-drenched foam that reached toward the sky.

When I returned to the cottage Micho was hovering above a gas stove. In a few minutes he handed me a plate of eggs, homemade bread, and potatoes.

"That'll be two pounds for the food," he declared gruffly, staring at me with those piercing ursine eyes.

We sat across from each other at a small wooden table and I mustered enough courage to ask him an inane question about his music. Suddenly he was opening up, telling me that he came from a long line of musicians. He could see that I was interested and began to sparkle. Yes, he and his brother Paddy were a dying breed of Irish *shenachie*—traveling minstrels and storytellers. Paddy played the fiddle and he the whistle and *bōdran.* The two of them knew over 500 traditional tunes that dated back hundreds of years and told many of the great stories of Ireland's past. The tunes had never been transcribed—something he hoped for dearly because he was growing old and had no offspring.

I replied that I might be able to help. Back in the States, I could make some inquiries at various universities. I was bound to find someone in ethnomusicology interested in helping him transcribe the tunes.

We agreed to stay in touch and I departed.

In the aftermath we exchanged letters (not easy because Micho was nearly illiterate). He sent me a copy of many of his tunes, and I wrote to King's College in Dublin about Micho and his music. In the mail came a reply that Micho Russell and his brother were legendary in the Irish music community. His music was considered valuable but past efforts to work with him had broken down because of misunderstandings about compensation.

A few years later I learned that Micho had died, but his wish had been fulfilled. A young American woman had contacted him, transcribed the tunes, and helped him record his story. I was much relieved.

Looking back on this, I realized that I was truly blessed to have had such an experience. If not for my willingness to spring for a few rounds of Guinness and throw a bit of caution to the wind it might never have happened. Buddha had never abandoned me and an apology was in order.

10
Recovering Buddha Nature

Step 9b. Rebalancing

Often problems on the road require more than troubleshooting. Something more fundamental may be awry which requires rebalancing and recovery of lost Buddha nature. Don't despair; even a Tibetan lama may occasionally need an attitude or outlook adjustment.

Your daily log and mandalas should provide you with indications of imbalance or signs that one or more of your Buddhas may have dropped off the back of your train. If you still aren't clear on who and what is missing, you might want to review your letters and other products of your deeper probing which should give you an indication of blind spots and unpracticed Buddha nature.

The spiritual path is not just a straight ascending road to happiness; there are many bumps and rises and dips on the road. Things may get more difficult before they become more coherent and tranquil. A great deal depends on what you've been ignoring in yourself. Some things inevitably must come up in order for you to know yourself and free yourself.

-LAMA SURYA DAS

Roll-Call to See Who Has Dropped off the Caboose

Below are some signs that may indicate one or more of my Buddhas has stepped off the caboose.

Table 10–1
Some Signs of Missing Buddhas

Buddha Nature	Signs that the Buddha is Missing
Mystic	No synchronicities; spinning mind; pinwheel anxieties; lack of meaningful experiences.
Healer	Recurrent illness, depression, persistent lack of energy; absence of compassion and empathy.
Explorer	No serendipity; lack of inventiveness or adventure; getting lost, making wrong turns and taking no delight in challenges of travel.
Enlightened Warrior	Repeated victimization; inability to follow anything through to completion; caught up in arguments; general sense that everything is a struggle.
Communicator	Inability to be understood or to make people connections; common arguments with travel companions; frustration in resolving conflicts.
Thinker	Repeatedly making same mistakes; absence of a plan; solutions that fall flat.
Artist	Flat artwork, ideas that lack novelty and insight, lack of artistic inspiration
Harlequin	Lack of drama, lack of laughter and joy

Any single sign may not necessarily be indicative of imbalance but a number of them in a particular category suggests that you are suppressing an important aspect of your higher self. Of course, you should also consider your baseline. Some people, for example, are constantly barraged by synchronicities. These may include the appearance of significant symbols, the uncanny arrival of a person you have just been thinking about, or some other improbable experience that can be meaningfully related to thought or action.

A friend of mine in Princeton experiences several synchronicities a week, even when he is not traveling. When we are together, a circus of bizarre events is bound to occur. If we are in a cafe talking about a friend, that friend is liable to appear in the doorway. If we're in a bookstore engaged in animated discussion on some esoteric topic, chances are good that a defining book will spontaneously drop from a shelf and land at our feet.

My own synchronicities increase markedly during trips. During my 1994 trip to Ireland and the Continent I counted twenty uncanny coincidences in a six-week period. These included repeated meetings with people I thought I had left behind.

One of the more improbable of these involved a young solicitor from Sri Lanka, whom I met on a long-haul train from Lucerne to Innsbruck. Over the course of three hours we engaged in an energetic discussion about culture and values. Just before Innsbruck he suggested I join him for a week of hiking but I declined, as I was intent on getting to Salzburg. I bid him goodbye thinking it unlikely that I would see him again.

Over the next several weeks my trip took several strange turns. Eventually I backtracked to Paris. One afternoon I was meandering through a crowded hallway of the Louvre when I heard an English voice calling out my name. I sloughed it off, certain that someone else was being hailed. After all, I knew only a handful of people on the Continent. I looked up to find the fellow from Sri Lanka.

We were both shocked by the improbability of this second encounter. Neither of us had mentioned the possibility of reversing course and coming to Paris, least of all to the Louvre and this particular hallway, which was crowded with at least 500 people. It was uncanny. My only explanation was that at some level the two of us had not completed our previous business, and yet I wasn't sure exactly what this was. We shared a cup of coffee and promised each other to stay in touch.

I've come to expect such experiences and know that their frequency reflects mindfulness, or in more concrete terms, a harmony between intention and action as well as attentiveness to inner Buddha nature. As described in chapter 4, this is the domain of Buddha as Mystic, which for me, especially on trips, tends to be a dominant identity and *modus operandi.* If synchronicities aren't occurring, I am usually not attentive enough and in most cases distracted by one or more of the common travel problems described in chapter 9.

A variety of signs and signals may indicate that one or more of the other Buddhas (besides Mystic) is being neglected. Continual health or energy problems usually point to a missing Healer and the need to bring such consciousness to daily activities. Perhaps you aren't taking care of yourself, perhaps ignoring the need for restful sleep or good nutrition. This isn't to suggest that all illness and disease is self-created, however, in most cases we affect our susceptibility because of inattention not only to our current condition but the environment in which we travel.

Whenever you are monitoring yourself, remember it is mindset that you are most interested in. The signs and signals of table 10-1 focus on the tangible effects of mindset. It is altogether possible that you are practicing a particular mindset but that nothing tangible has yet emerged. Outrageous sketches, lavish watercolors, and brilliant ideas aren't so much the proof of an energetic artist as perception, curiosity, and sensibility. In fact, Buddha as Artist may be hard at work, energetically integrating visual and tactile stimuli in a most creative way. Maybe you simply haven't recorded or expressed it.

One of my most artistic friends is a very eccentric fellow who may go several months at a time without painting, drawing, or inventing. And yet every time I run into him I am struck by the fact that he is the purest of artists. It's evident in the questions he asks, what he observes, and how he reacts to his surroundings. When he isn't creating he is gestating ideas and I can be sure that at some point down the road something very original will come to life.

If you have any doubts about a missing identity, play back in your mind the last few days on the road and ask yourself: What have I been thinking about? What amount of time have I spent entertaining the kinds of questions that Buddha as Artist (or another identity) brings to problem solving?

Finding Out How the Buddha Was Thrown from the Train

While sending out the rescue team to recover the missing Buddha, consider how he was lost in the first place. This will give you some assurance that you won't lose him again after he has returned.

As described in chapter 4, the loss of Buddha nature is almost always associated with shadow voices of limitation which erupt when we feel imperiled and stressed. Everyone has their own threshold for stress and discomfort and everyone has their own breaking point. We can be doing fine for quite some time, enduring the irritations of lost wallets and keys, overly soft mattresses and rude people, and then suddenly we snap. All at once we are cursing the universe, or maybe worse yet, taking it out on ourselves or those around us.

Most often we don't even realize what sets us off. Our triggers are subconscious. But if we take some time, we can excavate and understand what has happened: some things, some people, and some situations simply push our buttons and cause us to contract. The contraction and accompanying sense of peril cause us to lash out with aggression, shaming, manipulation, and other shadow behavior.

Over the course of my many extended trips to Europe I have gained increasing awareness of my own triggers. I know, for example, that especially when I am tired and after repeated nastiness from hotelkeepers, I grow intolerant of people who are uncivil and inhospitable. In such a context then, at the slightest provocation I let people know that I am not going to suffer their abuse.

Because of family history I know also that I tend to overreact to overbearing, controlling people, especially if I sense a manipulative intent. Whenever I meet someone like this I try harder to be forbearing, although in many instances I know that I am better off streaking for the nearest exit.

Know your own sensitivities and your ability to manage them and you save yourself and others a great deal of grief.

One way to heighten sensitivity to such problems is to draw them out. Recruit Buddha as Artist to create a map depicting the shadowland perils that set you off. Think of this as a game board for your travels through your own personal underworld. Show all the perils—trap doors, moats full of alligators, wicked witches, and vats of boiling oil. In creating your map you might also want to sketch out paths that will help you manage or avoid triggers.

If you are more linearly inclined you might want to construct your own version of table 10–2.

Table 10–2
Jim's Shadow Responses during Travel

Voice of Limitation	Situations That Provoke It	Blind Spot	Buddha Nature Abandoned
My French is too bad to speak to these people.	Intolerant responses from locals combined with fatigue.	Communicator can be understood even without perfect French.	Communicator
I refuse to be victimized by nasty or unruly people.	People crowding in lines in Metro or at airports.	Mystic doesn't really care. Realize that retaliating violates Spiritual Touchstone 9.	Enlightened Warrior, Mystic
I refuse to be gouged.	People asking too much for merchandise.	Communicator can negotiate with them; Mystic doesn't need to take offense.	Enlightened Warrior, Communicator
I refuse to ask for help.	Need for directions in a foreign city, but recent experience of being rebuffed (fatigue amplifies this).	Thinker knows that there are times when it makes sense to ask for help.	Thinker, Explorer

Excesses and Shadow

Besides triggers, another major reason why the Buddha ends up flying off the back of the train is excess. Strengths taken to extreme become weaknesses (Zylstra's Law). Enlightened Warriors, for example, are never very far from becoming destroyers. This is the case of the martial arts expert so caught up in warrior mentality and fighting skills that he becomes bully and victimizer. In effect, the training becomes a tool of ego, rather than spirit. Likewise, Thinker is never very far from becoming a doubting, authoritative cynic; Artist is never very far from becoming a dilettante; Explorer from becoming a reckless daredevil; and Mystic from becoming a judgmental, intolerant evangelist.

Retrieving Missing Buddhas

Drawing upon the ancient wisdom of Confucius recorded in the *Analects,* travel writer Phil Cousineau suggests five practices for travelers on spiritual journeys.

> *Practice the arts of attention and listening.*
> *Practice renewing yourself everyday.*
> *Practice meandering toward the center of every place.*
> *Practice the ritual of reading sacred texts.*
> *Practice gratitude and praise-singing.*

Each of these Confucian practices fortifies one or more of the Buddhas within. Each can help you regain Buddha nature that has been lost or underemphasized. Several such practices were discussed in chapters 5 and 6 which you might want to review (for example, fortifying and renewing your spirit and health). Some additional tips are suggested below.

Table 10–3
Ways to Awaken Buddha Nature

Buddha Nature	Specific Ways to Invoke It	First Signs of Awakening
Mystic	Review touchstones. More work on reflection. More gratitude. More laughter. Practice turning off the judgment and evangelism. Develop a thankful ritual.	Cessation of roller-coaster voices and emotions. More energy. A small synchronicity.
Artist	Sketch surroundings, faces. Study a piece of artwork in a museum and alter the pieces slightly.	An imaginative sketch.
Harlequin	Draw your current drama. Practice identifying dramas, actors, plot points, resolutions, complication. Imagine characters taking everything to extreme, —take the drama to a hilt. Describe a drama in a letter to self or friend.	Recognition of old pattern.
Explorer	Challenge yourself to come up with a solution to the current set-back; view the problem as opportunity.	You fix something; you have a satisfying adventure doing something new.

Table 10–3
Ways to Awaken Buddha Nature

Buddha Nature	Specific Ways to Invoke It	First Signs of Awakening
Communicator	Try your foreign language skills—avoid using English.	Someone actually understands your French. You make a personal connection.
Warrior	In heat of conflict you refuse to personalize an attack. You focus on energies available to you and try to turn negative into positive. Go running or exercise strenuously instead of succumbing to an addiction/appetite.	You make a decision and stick with it. You disarm someone's anger.
Healer	Detox; diet; exercise; Help someone with random act of kindness or generosity. Gift for a friend; show more compassion. Listen attentively to someone's problem.	You stick to your new diet or exercise regimen for two days in a row. You feel more energy; you avoid an addictive response.
Thinker	Take time to answer the questions of the Thinker in dealing with a problem. Practice deferring judgment and opinions until you are more certain. When asked for opinion, try replying, "I'm not sure; I don't know." Dive into a book and learn something.	You come up with a workable solution to a nontrivial problem.

Many of the practices are designed to manage or avoid triggers. I find that the work of Harlequin in uncovering and defining dramas helps me cope with people and situations that set me off. Offensive people are easier to tolerate when I realize why they provoke or irritate me.

Some triggers, however, can't be managed very easily and need to be avoided. I know, for example, that I can't be around smoke and cigarettes for very long before my breathing gets shallow and irritability sets in. Eventually the smoke affects my digestion, then my immune system. For all these reasons, Buddha as Healer draws the line on smoke. If I turn into a smoky pub or cafe, he blows me a kiss goodbye and declares that I am on my own.

Sometimes even a small gesture can be renewing. When a feeling of being spiritually stranded was coming over me during my 1998 trip to Brittany, I made a brief visit to Saint Corentin Cathedral in Quimper. There I lit a votive candle, fell into quiet meditation, and offered thanks for all the discovery and insights of my trip. As I withdrew into the radiant sunlight of the town square I felt much better.

Meandering about I spotted a doll shop and drew nearer. One doll in particular seemed to be staring at me and beckoning me to adopt her. I really didn't have room for her but I couldn't resist. I knew that she would be the perfect gift for a friend back home who had given me loving support during my mother's fatal illness. As it turned out the doll brightened and lightened the rest of my trip, making me feel good about the joy I would bring to my friend. The burden was no burden at all.

Meditation is also valuable for silencing static or other meaningless chatter. *Sunyata* or emptiness is a central teaching of Buddhism. Emptying meditation is simple and effective. It can be done anywhere at almost any time, and even a brief practice can be renewing. Try to find a place that will shelter you from distraction and allow you to fall within yourself. Begin relaxing by slowing and deepening your breathing. Breathe from your diaphragm and in and out through your nose. Exhale even more slowly than you inhale.

As you find a sustainable rhythm begin emptying yourself of all thought. Dissolve away all images; silence all noise; slow all motion. To facilitate this, repeat a simple mantra, such as the universal Tibetan phrase—*Ohm, mana padme hum* (translation: You are all that is within you. What is within you is what you are.).

Over the course of more and more practice you will discover that it is easier and easier to empty yourself. Breathing will also slow, distractions will lessen, and you will be able to compose and renew yourself with increasing ease.

Thoughts and Emotions

When people begin to meditate, they often say that their thoughts are running riot, and have become wilder than ever before. But I reassure them and say that it is a good sign. Far from meaning that your thoughts have become wilder, it shows that *you* have become quieter, and you are finally aware of just how noisy your thoughts have always been. Don't be disheartened or give up. Whatever arises, just keep being present, keep returning to the breath, even in the midst of all the confusion.

—Sogyal Rinpoche

On other occasions, regaining Buddha nature requires reengagement, or reentry into the flux. In 1996, I was on the Paris Metro and suffering a bit of angst about trying to communicate with the locals. I was also disoriented and in need of direction. Across from me was a beautiful young woman carrying a scruffy dog. We made eye contact and she smiled. My first thought was—lucky your French is so bad—you don't need to make a stumbling, pathetic attempt to talk to her. I took a deep breath and another internal voice erupted: "What's to lose? This trip is supposed to be about risk-taking. Step up and take a chance."

I smiled back at her and strung together a dim-witted but heroic question about her "petit chien," and suddenly we were conversing in French. She asked me where I was going and I pulled out my map and pointed to the scribbled address of a youth hostel. She declared that this was on the way to her apartment and that she would be happy to walk me there. A few minutes later we were on the street and talking art. She was an art student at the École des Beaux Arts and a member of a Paris troupe that regularly performed in public places. Before arriving at the hostel we set up a late-night rendezvous at one of her favorite cafes.

We had a smashing time and decided to spend more time together. In subsequent days we toured local galleries, visited cafes, and had dinner together with her friends. I experienced Paris in a way that few visitors ever have a chance. At the same time I renewed my sense of resourcefulness and self-confidence.

Of course, not all my risk-taking adjustments have worked out so gloriously. More than a few have been ungainful leaps in the dark that I was lucky to survive.

In 1994, I arrived by train in late evening in the spa town of Baden, Switzerland. I found a nearby cafe and consumed several hours in writing letters to friends. Suddenly I realized it was 9 P.M.—way too late to start thinking about a place to stay. I dashed off for a row of nearby hotels, hoping to get lucky.

No cheap rooms were available; however, one of the managers

knew of a hotel across town that usually had vacancies—an old spa hotel, something of a dinosaur, but inexpensive. He phoned ahead for me and told the manager that I would be there within the hour.

Unfortunately, in navigating to the hotel I took several wrong turns and arrived thirty minutes late. I found the lady manager in the second-floor lobby. She was scanning an old TV while stroking an infirm German shepherd. Right away I had a bad feeling about her. An incised scowl was on her brow and she refused to make eye contact.

"Too late," she declared without looking up.

I tried to explain my delay but she was unmoved. I smiled at her sweetly.

Her scowl only seemed to deepen.

"But you seem to have many vacant rooms." (The hotel was as empty as a mausoleum.)

"No one gets a room after 11 P.M."

"But you're my last resort," I answered feebly.

"You must leave. Out!" she declared, stirring the old dog to attention.

I started down the stairs to the first floor, but when I reached the landing three Buddhas erupted in sequence. First, came Buddha as Thinker: "If you don't stay here, you're out of luck. It's too late to find another place." Then came Buddha as Enlightened Warrior: "You're staying in this damn hotel, no matter what. Find a way."

I took three more steps and Explorer, master of resourcefulness, sounded off: "There's a restroom at the foot of the landing. Duck in there and she'll never notice."

Fortunately I had just enough time to make it. She locked the front door and limped back up the staircase. I huddled quietly in the dark recesses of the men's room and when my heart quieted I created a cushion to sleep on from the clothing in my backpack. I wasn't going to be comfortable but at least I wouldn't freeze to death.

Later that night I sneaked back to the lobby and returned with blankets. I might have slept except for fear of being rousted by the old dog. Early in the morning I heard him barking and held my breath. I could hear his paws tattooing the linoleum floor as he drew near.

Miraculously he turned tail. I wondered if Buddha had come to my protection, perhaps covering my scent with that of a dead cat. Then again, the hotel reeked so thoroughly of mold that only a super-hound would have been able to penetrate it and pick up my scent.

Not much later, though it seemed like a long time, the manager unlocked the front door and turned away. She was barely out of view when I streaked for the door. I reached the street and smiled back with relief. I had survived and simultaneously executed a most resourceful coup. In the aftermath I wondered if it was the coup of a lunatic. Adventures like this I could do without.

11

Bringing the Lessons Home

*B*uddha as Harlequin is trickster, master of irony and paradox, lover of laughter and a good prank. He is pleased to inform you that you have been tricked. You have been at home from the very beginning. Your first and last steps have been down a familiar path. The dramas you have played out are the perennial dilemmas of self-identity, faith and doubt, the inescapablity of mortality, and the puzzle of tapping inner powers to find a way out of the dark.

> We shall not cease from
> exploration
> And the end of all our exploring
> Will be to arrive where
> we started
> And know the place for
> the first time.
>
> *- T.S. ELIOT*

The adventures of travel are the adventures of everyday life, only taken to extremes and condensed into a shorter period of time. As a result, when you are on the road you are really at home; when you are at home you are really on the road.

The lesson goes deeper still—everything you have done, every adjustment you have made over the course of your trip is already a part of your repertoire because it was within you from the beginning.

OHM MANA PADME HUM.
(You are all that is within you.
What is within you is what you are.)

The challenge is to make sure that you don't miss what was really going on during your trip and the ordinary and not-so-ordinary magic performed by your Buddhas.

Step 10. Debriefing

Your debriefing is your bird's-eye view of your dramas. It is your thoughtful attempt to act as witness to your experiences and draw out essential insights. It should focus on the correspondence between intention and experience, including the story of how you responded to impediments and opportunities.

The results of my own debriefings are recorded in Section 4 of my journal and usually take around five pages. I address the following points.

Points to Address in Debriefing
—Intentions and Objectives Realized
—Dramas
—Themes and Insights
—Capacities Tapped/Untapped
—Unfinished Business
—Resolutions

I usually begin with a point-by-point review of the objectives recorded in the front of my journal. Most of the time I discover that what I was looking for changed, and several of the stated objectives gave way to others. Few trips square with original intentions, expectations, and plans.

Your original intention might have been rest and relaxation from burn-out, but once you arrived at Côte d'Azur or the Riviera, it all changed. Perhaps you visited someone who sparked your sense of adventure and before you knew it you had signed on for a sailing adventure in the eastern Mediterranean.

An outer adventure might just as easily turn into inner adventure, for example, to deal with your own grief, which was the case for me in 1998. Reviewing the changes in your intentions can be valuable in

Table 11–1
Drama's and Opportunities of Jim's Trip

Drama	Triggers and Contributing Factors	Outcome	Notes
Locked out of hostel in Brienz	Poor communication with hostel manager. Refusal to yell for help.	Slept outside.	
Romantic involvement with Annemarie that turned into roller-coaster relationship	Immediate connection upon first meeting. Spontaneity and willingness to open up to each other.	Painful distortions. Manipulation and finally disengagement.	
Healing from pneumonia in Denmark	Weak immune system. Carousing.	Spontaneous healing. Greater faith in higher powers.	
Connection with Bernadette in Paris	Desire to talk. Willingness to test French.	Friendship, adventure as a result of putting myself out despite apprehensions.	
Conversation with psychologist from Liechtenstein	Shared compartment on train. Mutual willingness to talk.	Deep conversation/ connection.	
Trip to Venice	Prompted by awareness of own grieving. Spontaneous healing. Ability to take train to Venice because of Eurail Pass.	Rich art experience. Communing with Mom's spirit.	

clarifying and defining insights.

Not all your insights will be obvious. Many of the pearls come from reviewing the dramas of your trip. To facilitate the review, I created a table in which I describe the basic dramas, triggers, and outcomes. Table 11–1 is an example of one such table that I filled in after a trip.

Although it is tempting to jump directly to insights, I like to hold back until after I have listed and described all the dramas. This allows me to see commonalities and patterns, which lead to discoveries I might have missed.

I also like to create a table such as the one shown in table 11–2 in which I probe the spiritual side of the journey and identify some of the overarching themes.

While dramas tend to be very specific and concrete—romance, an outdoor test of survival, and so on, themes express the more fundamental dynamic, such as risk-taking, proving resourcefulness, trying to be self-sufficient, trying to be open and understanding. Themes can be both positive and negative or simply neutral characterizations of what was apparently going on. Additional themes from recent trips have included those listed below.

Examples of Themes
- looking for love in the wrong places
- compulsive attempts to prove resourcefulness
- extreme efforts to validate self-worth
- putting oneself in harm's way (daredevil behavior)
- relying on others to rescue me rather than fending for myself
- perfectionism (inadequate accommodations, intolerable behavior of others, and so on)
- overreaction to abusive behavior (taking it too personally)
- the workings of grace

Table 11–2
Themes and Insights from Dramas on the Road

Drama	Themes	Buddha	Insight	Notes
Locked out of hostel in Brienz	Self-sufficiency	Explorer	Discovered power of toilet paper as insulation. Craziness of not crying out for help (ego).	
Painful involvement with Annemarie	Illusions in their many forms; *zeitgeist* and myth	Thinker	Need to think more about consequences and recognize romantic myopia during travel. False equation between being earthy and spiritual.	
Healing from pneumonia in Denmark	Spirit of place	Healer and Mystic	Affirm touchstones, especially Touchstone 1.	Breath of life
Connection with Bernadette in Paris	Letting go Openness. Risking rejection	Communicator	Importance of risking rejection if hope to make contact with others. Affirm ability to avoid pitfalls of erotic attraction.	

Table 11–2 (continued)
Themes and Insights from Dramas on the Road

Drama	Themes	Buddha	Insight	Notes
Connection with Psychologist from Liechtenstein	Surface illusions Distortion	Communicator, Mystic	Affirm need to go beyond looks in judging others. Importance of for-bearance.	
Trip to Venice	Art as tonic	Mystic	Affirm ability to commune with Mom's spirit. Affirm gifts of vitality and artistic expression from mother. Recognize that grieving has own timetable.	Symbol of water as it relates to spirit
Connections on the road in western Ireland	Openness to others	Mystic, Harlequin	Increased interest in Buddhism and Eastern spirituality. Role of mind as the author of experi-ence.	Monks everywhere

Quite often the themes of a trip are expressed by recurrent symbols. This is the world of Jungian archetypes. I have noted a few symbols in column 5, "Notes."

On my trip to Ireland in 1994, my trip took a strange turn after the spirituality conference in Killarney. While traveling north through Listowel, Dingle, and several villages in County Clare, I noticed one monk after another. In each instance, the fellow would slip away just as I focused on him—vanishing behind a city wall, into a crowd, or inside a bus. I couldn't help but think of those teasing cameos by Alfred Hitchcock in all his movies—one second he's there; the next he's gone.

I was ready to write these off as simple coincidences when I was picked up on the road just north of Listowel. The driver was as an affable Aussie looking for someone to talk to. Just outside of Dingle, I detached from conversation and gazed out on a barren expanse of land skirting the ocean. A ground fog had descended across a thalo-green field that stretched to a rugged megalith. I turned slightly and noticed a blur of saffron. A monk, perhaps a hundred yards away, seemed to be skipping toward the rock outcropping. He disappeared before I could get the Aussie to notice him.

The next day I stopped in Doolin for dinner. At a country restaurant a gregarious waitress questioned me about my trip. I blurted out that everywhere I turned were elusive Buddhist monks playing a mischievous game of appearing and then disappearing before they could be recognized.

She was quick to reply that Sean the chef would be interested in this. Just a few days ago he had commented on seeing a Tibetan monk.

Sean appeared and right away we achieved a rapport. He was very voluble and likeable. He listened attentively to my unabashed discharge about the slippery monks. When I stopped to see if he thought I was a complete lunatic, he smiled mischievously and replied in a thick Irish accent:

"Ah, Jimmy, me boy it doesn't really surprise me a bit. These things are quite common in County Clare. In fact, it was just the other day when me and a few of the boys were driving the truck down the road to Ennis and suddenly we look over to our left in the other lane and this monk is streaking by us lickity-split."

"All the monks I see are on foot. Not a one was driving a car."

"Twern't no car," he replied with a twinkle in his eye.

I probably should have added an additional drama to my list—shined by local Celts.

Just because an image sticks in your mind or obsesses you, it doesn't necessarily hold great meaning. Still, much like a recurrent dream, a persistent image or symbol can reflect ongoing processing by the subconscious. My monk episode, I believe, was about a developing mindset, a reorientation-in-progress toward Eastern philosophy and spirituality. It hadn't yet surfaced as intention or conviction. With greater reflection, I realized that this was one of the subtle *sub-rosa* dramas of my trip. Certainly after the conference in Killarney I was much more sensitive to the ways in which Buddhism and Eastern philosophy could add joy and purpose to daily living and help me understand my own personal struggles.

The end-product of table 11–2, captured in column 4, are your insights. Additional insights from recent trips have included the following:

- affirmation of Touchstone 7 (Individual as Member of a Greater Family/Collective)

- elaboration on Touchstone 3 (Indispensability of Risk), whereby I distinguish between healthy and unhealthy risk-taking
- ways I can fortify body and spirit away from home
- the importance of accepting others on their terms; adjusting to local customs
- ways to practice art without all the usual tools
- discovery that you can dry wet shoes overnight by stuffing them with newspaper

As you can see, I leave room for the occasional thunderbolt having no real spiritual value (for example, how to dry wet shoes with newspaper).

If you can stand back and look objectively at each drama, you can usually discover a role played by mindset, including practiced or unpracticed Buddha nature. Buddhists believe that mindset is behind all experience, particularly ego attachments, distortion/ignorance, and extreme shadow responses. (These are sometimes referred to as the three poisons.)

Perhaps a series of debacles in trying to catch trains and find accommodations in Paris was triggered by my trying to prove resourcefulness or refusing to admit the need for help. Perhaps the drama of a travel romance revolved around a completely crazy illusion about foreigners or maybe a misguided notion that such involvement would be without emotional cost.

In looking for insights I usually ask myself what I did to recover Buddha nature when it seemed hopelessly lost. I also look at the ways in which an apparent disaster provoked a discovery about identity or balancing that might empower me in other situations, on the road or at home.

Transitions

Chances are good that you will be returning home to a chaos that equates to an Italian train station during a general strike—everything gridlocked; everyone clamoring for help in a strange language; and no room to breathe and think. A pile of bills may be waiting for you; your phone machine is apt to be clogged; and even your most respected friends and family may be acting like abandoned codependents.

If this is what you come home to, you may be beset by a sense of despair and inertia, a feeling of losing all the freedom and possibility that you touched, albeit briefly, on your trip. I am one of those people who falls into a virtual *bardo** when my trip ends, stuck between the life I have been living and the life I am not yet willing to embrace. I tend to linger at a local cafe and stare wistfully at travel photographs. Under the influence of straight espresso, I plot out impractical escapes to the airport and schemes for supporting myself while I am away.

I have come to realize that most of the letdown results from believing that travel ends simply because you have returned home. The truth is you are still traveling but under different conditions. Mindset is the issue.

Most of us need to let go of the illusion that life is only rewarding elsewhere or in someone else's shoes. This is simply another voice of limitation and a cop-out. Almost always the present holds some opportunity for engaging adventure that challenges Buddha nature.

Henry Miller as Mystic cuts to the heart of the matter:

> When you find you can go neither backward nor forward, when you discover that you are no longer able to stand, sit or lie down, when you children have died of malnutrition and your aged parents have been sent to the poorhouse or the gas chamber, when you realize that you can neither write nor not write, when you are convinced that all the exits are blocked, you either take to believing in miracles

*In Tibetan Buddhism a transitional state of spiritual being.

or you stand still like the hummingbird. The miracle is that the honey is always there, right under your nose, only you were too busy searching elsewhere to realize it. The worst is not death but being blind, blind to the fact that everything about life is in the nature of the miraculous.

Buddha nature allows us to transcend our blind spots and see the opportunity in present circumstance. A barren landscape may suddenly appear as a gold-tinged, honey field of possibility. Opportunities abound. The limitation we saw before is replaced by abundance.

In order to sustain the divinity you have experienced on your trip, commit yourself to continuing your voyage with the mindset you practiced as an enlightened traveler.

Review of Intentions

The transition won't be so full of anxiety if what you are doing in daily life is in line with your spirit and sense of personal meaning. If you feel that your intentions are now different than during your travels, and you are not sure of your path, then perhaps it is time to reconsider where you are headed and whether you are practicing the wholeness of heart and spirit that you are capable of.

You may want to leap directly to intentions and life goals, but I recommend that instead you recapitulate the steps of your trip, described in previous chapters. First, take a look at your spiritual touchstones. No doubt they need a bit of revision after all you have experienced with vanishing and reappearing Buddhas, inscrutable synchronicities, and struggles with shadow impulses. Revisions are always in order after a significant travel adventure, be it disastrous or divine.

Touchstones, Personal Voice, and Dharma

Remember that your touchstones are your fundamental spiritual truths. They not only express spiritual laws but how you relate to your reality as a spiritual being. In the famous Heart Sutra, the Buddha describes how his own dharma, or middle-way, sprang forth from his experiences in the forest confronting shadow.

First, he had to abandon the extreme abnegation and mortification that the zealots around him claimed was necessary to attain enlightenment.

After nearly starving himself, he felt no gain. His heart was numb, his body feeble. He only began to fill with life when he realized he was not a slave to dogma, that he was a spiritual being defined by more than his ability to endure suffering. It dawned on him that such austere abnegation was really only a different kind of bodily indulgence. Practicing compassion and mindfulness promised a deeper connection to the divine.

The brightness of this realization only intensified as he came to understand the workings of intention, the need for responsible self-acceptance, service, and commitment to truth, however unpopular. Five hundred years later in Jerusalem, Christ would go through a similar struggle with authority to practice his own divine way.

In redefining and revising your own touchstones, try to separate your own heartfelt beliefs from the views and values of others. Reflect on what you know about the immortal spirit based upon your own dark moments in the forest. Also consider those moments during your travels when gratitude and joy billowed your sails and you extended that gratitude to others. Recall how this made you feel at peace with your surroundings and connected you to kindred souls and larger community.

Buddha Nature, Attachment, and Freedom

Do you remember the discussion in chapter 10 which addressed the difficulties of maintaining balance? You were asked to identify triggers of shadow behavior. In the process you may have even mapped out pitfalls along your spiritual path. These may have included the people and situations that provoke voices of limitation and shrinking faith and inner divinity.

At the root of shadow behavior is fear of suffering and fear of death. We try to protect ourselves because we don't want to suffer and we cave in to our apprehensions that death is final.

When you think about these fears they begin to deflate. Suffering takes different forms but so much of it is psychic and emotional and caused by ego attachments. We suffer because our ego is invested in comfort, status, and values defined by others. Our lack of self-authority causes us to buy into values that measure our worth by our personal pile of possessions, our degrees from prestigious universities, our trophy spouses, and our perceived status or popularity. Our kids mirror our craziness by valuing designer labels, begging for the latest pair of Air Jordans, or parroting the right cool in order to be accepted by peers.

The psychic misery manifests itself physically: so many of our chronic physical problems, be they allergies, diabetes, attention deficit disorders, recurring bouts of the flu, are affected, if not caused by, perceived failures or fears of them. Disease, in effect, becomes a manifestation of dis-ease.

The irony is that security is rarely the real issue. Not having expensive and showy possessions never jeopardizes us, nor does lack of popularity or status. In fact, if security were really an issue, why wouldn't we invest in our creativity, our resourcefulness, our health, and our compassion? Aren't these, in fact, the only capacities that remedy our perceived shortcomings and give us defense against real shortage and limitation?

Stop and consider how many of your motivations have anything to do with fundamental needs. It can be sobering, especially if you are honest. Be sure to consider such "needs" as the car with the right accessories, computers with enough memory and speed to perform all conceivable operations, make-up to camouflage aging, and possibly cosmetic surgery to prop up sex appeal and enhance youthfulness.

Henry Miller had more to say on the topic of security, conformity and self-authority: "The language of society is conformity; the language of the creative individual is freedom."

Life becomes a living hell as long as we refuse to acknowledge and express our creative and compassionate potential, as long as we allocate our energy to measuring up and aggrandizing. The truth is that almost no one ever measures up and everyone is beset by feelings of incompleteness and lack of meaning. Gorgeous models are worried about fat; successful businessmen feel diminished because their portfolio isn't performing as well as Gates, Allen, and Buffet. One of the imperatives of Buddha nature is to quit kidding ourselves that everything will be okay if only we hit the lottery or someone with power comes along to discover us. If we were discovered or did hit the jackpot without a change in consciousness, the gain would be questionable. Most probably we would only develop more expensive anxieties, insecurities, and feelings of incompleteness. Mind leads; external reality follows.

Behind our desperation we all have a soul memory. It is the faint remembrance of satisfaction, immeasurable satisfaction, gained in offering someone a helping hand, creating something that we thought was beyond us, committing ourselves to integrity and truth, and discovering that it adds peace to our life, even though it may not result in a material payoff.

One of the problems with this soul memory is that it is imperfect. Our view of the past is colored and distorted. Through blurred lenses we are easily confused by substances and ego-fixes that temporarily gratify rather than add peace, composure, and self-awareness.

A few years back the concept of flow was in vogue. Books came out in bundles about flow that could be gained from running, climbing mountains, purifying through austere diets, and ingesting exotic plants from South America. So much was made of the possibilities and the biochemical mechanisms that few people asked whether there was any real difference between one flow state and another.

We now understand that there is. We know that most of these states are only cheap and weak facsimiles of the unitive consciousness experienced in meditation or through other mindful practices. For a brief moment we can indulge our narcissistic impulses and feel that we are "king (or queen) of the world," but the feelings ebb, and without any gain in self-awareness we are no better off. In fact, in most cases we are only stirred to ride a wilder roller-coaster.

Mindful practices are different. Although they may lift us up, they also modulate the highs and lows, delivering us from our manic and compulsive mood swings.

They also give us space. This is critical. Only if we give ourselves space for contemplation and reflection are we able to invoke our Buddha nature. Space provides the opportunity to invoke the silent witness—and then to ask the critical question, "What in Buddha's name was I thinking about?" If this question never pops up, you can be sure there is not enough spiritual margin in your life.

Fear of death is the other great anxiety that causes the rat to run himself ragged on the metal wheel. When we believe that our days are numbered, desperation sets in. We drive faster, we take less time to eat, we navigate fewer of the scenic routes, and we grow impatient with anyone depriving us of our precious time.

It is not hard to imagine how we might be affected if a genie suddenly appeared and granted everyone an extra hundred years and a dose of youthfulness. Think of the possibilities. If you lacked adequate education, perhaps you would go back to school and fill in the gaps. Maybe you would make a few aimless excursions into art or glass blowing. Perhaps you would feel less rushed to find a suitable mate, to start a family, or to position yourself for the climb up a career ladder.

There can be little doubt that our desperation is at least partially driven by a runaway hourglass.

Suppose, however, that you were assured of coming back. Not only that, suppose your rushed, half-baked, desperate choices affected your next life—that they were carried forward as unfinished business which you had to face. This might include obligations you had dodged and people you had wronged, like that poor sot on whom you once pawned off that broken-down Chrysler that was blowing blue smoke. It's a sobering thought. Certainly if Karma applied you would want to make sure that your next incarnation wasn't simply a return to make good on past debts, to atone and compensate. You would certainly spend more time "doing things right" in the first place.

Of course, you might say that this is all well and good, but what evidence do I have that I am coming back? I don't have a compelling answer to that, only that this kind of knowledge transcends logic and empirical method. We aren't persuaded of the truth by data or force of argument; we simply *know* it. The recognition comes in a feeling of perfect harmony in the same way that we feel the resonance of beautiful music, art, or a passage of powerful writing.

Witnessing a spiritual self that transcends the body is this kind of bell-ringing experience. Unfortunately you will never hear any ringing bells unless you are listening. Those who are closed to the idea, never experience it.

How Can a Spiritual Being Survive on the Earth Plane?

The guru often advises the student to let go of attachments, but this is always easier said than done. Outside of a monastery we have to pay mortgages, support ourselves and family, and negotiate all the other stresses of modern life. At times it seems that you almost need to be a lama to deal with the traffic congestion, the harassment by phone solicitors, and the countless other people trying to sell you something you don't need. The stresses are greater still if suddenly you are laid off, caught up in a family health emergency, find parents suddenly dependent on you, or discover your child has fallen in with the wrong crowd at school.

Almost all of us would like a greater ability to cope, a bit more forbearance and spirituality, but we don't have the option of traveling to India to find enlightenment, as the Buddha did. Even if we tried, how far would we get?

Even if we passed customs and made it to the Bodhi Tree, what chance would we have for quiet meditation? No doubt we would be interrupted by a crowd of lawyers, bill-collectors and more salespeople trying to get a piece of us. I doubt that any of them would accept *"Ohm mani padme hum"* as sufficient answer.

Nowadays the notion of a middle path means balancing the needs for a spiritual inner life with the demands and responsibilities of living in modern society.

Assuming that over the course of your trip you have gained some experience in lightening your load and realized the benefits of it, consider doing something similar in daily life to lighten your spiritual burden. Ask yourself what ego attachments you can spare that will make life more spiritual, that will allow you to find closer harmony between high intention and how you invest yourself.

Some monitoring might be in order along the lines of the mindful practices of your trip. Pose the same basic questions. Ask yourself what occupies your daily energy and thought? Consider how much time you devote to property maintenance and to indulgent, roller-coaster behavior, rather than to higher self or Buddha nature. Be sure to account for compensations—time you spend unwinding from the roller-coaster (for instance, a drink here or there, an appointment to the chiropractor for an adjustment, and so forth).

When most people do this they realize how little time and effort they really give to higher self. One thing is certain: mindfulness is next to impossible if you don't provide the space.

Facing the Emptiness

One of the reasons we stay on the roller-coaster is because we are terrorized by the prospect of silence and emptiness. We think of them as a horrific vacuum in which life ceases. Our worst fear is that once we remove the motion and clutter of living, strip away the addictions and compulsions, set aside the obligations, there will be nothing left, absolutely nothing.

Our travel experience can give us something valuable to draw on in response to this terror.

Recall the moments that you were stranded in those airports and train stations. Recall the interludes when the spinning stopped and you momentarily surrendered to the higher forces around you. This may have come on a road twenty miles from nowhere after your car gave out, or perhaps in an Irish pub where you stopped for a beer and puzzled over your disorientation.

With no hopes and no prospects what happened? In that empty gap of consciousness, close to total surrender, you experienced the stillness of the hummingbird. Perfect serene quiet. A precious moment in the vacuum when nothing happened, not even an anxious twinge. And then out of the gap came an utterly absurd idea—perhaps a quick fix to your car problem or a silly way to regain your bearings. You thought a bit more and then suddenly your mind was churning with honeyed variations on that original idea that weren't so crazy and impractical. They might have even seemed inspired. That inner voice was the Buddha offering a helping hand. You thought you were alone, but it was illusion. Buddha never left you. He was simply waiting in the silence for you to invite his help.

If you are unconvinced of this divine presence and feel the need for reassurance and renewal, consider again the prescriptions of Phil Cousineau:

> *Practice the arts of attention and listening.*
> *Practice renewing yourself every day.*
> *Practice meandering toward the center of every place.*
> *Practice the ritual of reading sacred texts.*
> *Practice gratitude and praise-singing.*

Of all the renewing practices, few are so powerful as spreading love and compassion. Fortunately the possibilities are endless. The world is full of people who need a helping hand. Be sure, however, that in giving you attach no strings. Expect nothing in return and practice nonjudgment.

Dramatic Imperatives

Your travel journey started with an exhortation to embrace the unfolding drama. The drama continues now that you are home. It is a drama of interaction with friends, family, and work cohorts, with strangers, bill collectors, people that manipulate you, people that love you, people that praise you, people that push your buttons, people that are trying to sell you something.

As with your trip, the dramas of everyday life are almost always about dealing with shadow, dealing with impulses to protect ourselves due to some misperceived peril or shortage. The problem is daunting but only overwhelming if we hold ourselves to an impossible standard—to rid and lid our capacities for violence, excessive judgment, and negative feelings. If we set out on this path, we never succeed. We only grow more frustrated and typically deny, avoid, and project.

When we project, and we are all guilty of that, we lash out at others as a result of self-dissatisfaction. Of course, we have our rationalizations. We justify our defensiveness by simply refusing to be victimized by others who are unfair or trying to take advantage of us. But how often is this the case? And how often does it really matter what people say about us or do to us? Most of the time we are simply better off by letting the negative energy pass and viewing someone else's wrath and harmfulness as their issue not ours, their attachment and ignorance that we don't need to be affected by.

Above all, when you find yourself in a situation like this, stay focused. Remember that what is most important is your spirit, which is safe from the slights of others. Only you can damage that. In the end, lashing out only makes us feel worse about ourselves and alienates us from our divinity.

If you fall into the trap, don't despair. The drama of travel is always about recovery from mistakes, always about glorious imperfection. All of our Buddhas are prone to pitfalls. In Paris they often stuff themselves with almond croissants and suffer from bellyaches. In Galway they drink too much Guinness and might even be drawn into a bar fight. In Germany they make derisive comments about accordion music or fall prey to the charms of enchanting Bavarian nature-girls.

Fortunately all of the Buddhas are redeemed by their commitment to self-awareness and responsibility. Each one is willing to cast away illusion, confront the truth, and try again with a bit more mindfulness. The nice thing about traveling with such a sidekick is that second chances abound and with them the promise of a more fulfilling and meaningful journey.

Unnumbered Notes

p. 131 from Henry Miller, *Stand Still Like the Hummingbird,* p. 27 (New Directions, 1962).

p. 133 from John Welwood, *Journey of the Heart,* p. 138 (Harper Perennial, 1990).

p. 135 from Henry Miller, *Tropic of Cancer,* p. 1 (Grove Press, 1961).

p. 135 from Henry Miller, *The Cosmological Eye,* p. 2 (New Directions, 1939).

p. 149 from Henry Miller, *Tropical Cancer,* p. 1 (Grove Press, 1961).

p. 168 from Phil Cousineau, *The Art of Pilgrimage,* p. 2 (Conari Press, 1998).

p. 172 from Sogyal Rinpoche, *The Tibetan Book of Living and Dying,* p. 73 (HarperSanFrancisco, 1994).

p. 187 from Henry Miller, *Stand Still Like the Hummingbird,* p. ix (New Directions, 1962).

Recommended Reading

Bensen, Herbert. *Timeless Healing.* New York: Scribner, 1996.

Berman, Morris. *Coming to Our Senses.* New York: Bantam, 1990.

Chopra, Deepak. *Quantum Healing.* New York: Bantam, 1990.

Cousineau, Phil. *The Art of Pilgrimage.* Berkeley, California: Conari Press, 1998.

Dossey, Larry. *Recovering the Soul.* New York: Bantam, 1989.

Frankl, Victor. *The Unheard Cry for Meaning.* New York: Washington Square Press, 1984.

Golan, Ralph. *Optimum Wellness.* New York: Ballantine Books, 1999.

Goleman, Daniel. *Vital Lies, Simple Truth.* New York: Simon and Schuster, 1985.

Goswami, Amit. *The Self-Aware Universe: How Consciousness Creates the Material World,* Los Angeles: Jeremy Tarcher, 1993.

Greenberg, Michael. *Paradox and Healing.* Victoria, Canada: Meridian House, 1992.

Grof, Christina. *The Thirst for Wholeness: Attachment, Addiction and the Spiritual Path.* San Francisco: HarperSan Francisco, 1993.

Harman, Willis. *Higher Creativity: Liberating the Unconscious for Breakthrough Insights.* Los Angeles: Jeremy Tarcher, 1984.

Hixson, Lex. *Coming Home.* Burdett, New York: Larson Publications, 1978.

Joy, W. Brugh. *Joy's Way.* Los Angeles: Jeremy Tarcher, 1979.

Kopp, Sheldon. *If You Meet the Buddha on the Road, Kill Him.* New York: Bantam, 1972.

———. *Guru-Metaphors from a Psychotherapist.* Palo Alto, California: Science and Behavior Books, 1971.

Kornfield, Jack. *A Path with Heart.* New York: Bantam, 1993.

Kumar, Satish. *Path Without Destination.* New York: William Morrow, 1972.

Lama Surya Das. *Awakening to the Sacred.* New York: Broadway Books, 1999.

———. *Awakening the Buddha Within.* New York, Broadway Books, 1997.

Levine, Steven. *Who Dies.* New York: Doubleday, 1982.

Lowen, Alexander, M.D. *The Spirituality of the Body.* New York: MacMillan, 1990.

May, Rollo. *The Courage to Create.* New York: Bantam, 1976.

Miller, Henry. *Big Sur and the Oranges of Hieronymous Bosch.* New York: New Directions, 1956.

———. *The Cosmological Eye.* New York: New Directions, 1939.

———. *The Paintings of Henry Miller: Paint as You Like and Die Happy.* New York: Chronicle Books, 1973.

———. *Stand Still Like the Hummingbird.* New York: New Directions, 1962.

Peat, F. David. *Synchronicity: The Bridge Between Matter and Mind.* New York: Bantam, 1988.

Pierrakos, Eva. *The Pathwork of Self-Transformation.* New York: Bantam, 1990.

Rinpoche, Soygal. *The Tibetan Book of Living and Dying.* San Francisco: HarperSanfrancisco, 1994.

Shainberg, Lawrence. *Ambivalent Zen.* New York: Vintage Books, 1955.

Talbott, Michael. *The Holographic Universe.* New York: Harper Perennial, 1991.

Thich Nhat Hanh. *Peace in Every Step: The Path of Mindfulness in Everyday Life.* New York: Bantam, 1991.

Walsh, Roger, and Francis Vaughn, editors. *Paths Beyond Ego, The Transpersonal Vision.* Los Angeles: Jeremy Tarcher, 1993.

Watts, Alan. *The Way of Liberation.* New York: Weatherhill Press, 1983.

Welch, Holmes. *Taoism-The Parting of the Way.* Boston: Beacon Press, 1957. 37.

Welwood, John. *Journey of the Heart.* New York: Harper Perennial, 1990.

Wilber, Ken. *Grace and Grit.* Boston: Shambhala, 1991.

———. *Sex Ecology and Spirituality.* Boston: Shambhala, 1995.

Zukav, Gary. *The Seat of the Soul.* New York: Simon and Schuster, 1989.

Index

fear–based, 44
Harlequin archetype, 39, 44, 177
inner and outer, 8, 10
of journeys, 10, 12, 43–44, 197–98
themes, 181–83
zooming in and out, 131–32
dukkha, 18

ego, 192 (*see also* shadow and projections)

flow, 192
formatting your journal:
  artwork, 23
  notebooks, 22
  sections in journal, 21
  space, 21
  (*see also* method for journal keeping)
fortifying spirit, 36, 106–7, 196

grace
  "Amazing Grace," 135
  as divine blessing, 9

Hinduism
  Brahman, 41
  five bodies, 33
health
  barometric ratings, 25, 123
  chi, 136
  fatigue, 106
  feet, 106
  organizations for help, 104–5
  persistent problems, 152–53
  preventing illness, 36, 103–4
  stresses of travel, 102–3
  water, 105

insights from travel, 183–86
intentions
  deeper, 81–82, 154
  general travel interests, 75, 79, 81
  identification, 80

objectives, 81
process, 82, 84
review in debriefing, 188
romance, 79–80
shaping during trip, 85
Gary Zukav, 75

journal keeping
  for business, 13
  for consciousness, 11
  guidelines, 116–20
  impediments and dramas, 12
  minimal entry, 120–22
  notebook criteria, 18, 20
  playfulness, 127
  solo and tour travel, 13

loss of documents, 111

meditation, 38, 172, 194 (*see also* reflection)
meeting people, 113–14, 153–54
method for journal keeping:
  address book, 29
  barometers, 25–26, 122–24
  budget, 21, 28
  calendars, 24–25
  daily log, 22, 29, 115–32
  debriefing, 178–79
  formatting, 21–29
  guidelines for entries, 116–20
  letters, 29
  mandalas, 21, 27–28, 48–49, 66
  photographs, 28
  steps, 11, 14
  time requirements, 14
  tools, 14, 100–101
  touchstones, 31–46

Nuñez Cabeza de Vaca, 31

objectives
  general, 80–83